Little Black Heifer

Little Black Heifer

Latonia D. Artis, MS in Psychology

The author has tried to recreate events, locations, and conversations from his/her memories of them. To stay anonymous, the author has altered names of people and places. He/she may also have changed identifying characteristics and details such as physical attributes, occupations, and places of residence.

Copyright © 2014 by Latonia Artis
First published in 2025 by LA Publishing
lapublishing52@gmail.com

All rights reserved. No part of this book may be reproduced or transmitted in any form or by any means, electronic or mechanical, including photocopying, recording, or any information storage and retrieval system, without permission in writing from the author.

ISBN: 978-1-7365584-1-6 – Paperback
ISBN: 978-1-7365584-2-3 – Hardcover
eISBN: 978-1-365584-0-9 – eBook

Printed in the United States of America

∞This paper meets the requirements of ANSI/NISO Z39.48-1992 (Permanence of Paper)

061925

Preface

I DEDICATE THIS book to all of God's People, whether Believers or non-believer. This book will not be the average read. Be prepared to experience a variety of emotions: laughter, joy, amazement, sadness, encouragement, strength, regret, and more.

God blessed me to be a vessel to take on burdens of others in his way for the healing of a multitude of people of all social classes, age, color, and beliefs. He is a wonder in my soul and others. I have been privileged to have individuals cross my path that added to my spiritual growth, whether positive or negative. The adverse events encountered with certain individuals blessed me so. Gold nuggets are what I have taken from not-so-good relationships. I considered them treasures that I will value for the rest of my life.

The individuals familiar with me and those who have known me always encouraged me to author a book about my life experiences. They said if I authored a book about my life experiences, it would help people. My response has been, "Everyone has a testimony and has been through things in life. What makes me any different?" My comment came from a place where I am equal to those that have ever been through challenging life events that people recover from, and others do not. My comfort zone is just praying, encouraging, providing aid to those that God sends my way at an appointed time. That is my passion for God's people.

I hope and pray that this book that I pour my heart into will help people overcome the same battles that they keep experiencing repeatedly. I pray that yokes "be broken" over your lives permanently. Some would say that Yokes can "be broken" but can re-surface again. A Wise individuals say that "the yoke was never broken in the first place." Well, God's word tells stories of great people of the statue that still battled with low self-esteem, an insufficient measure of faith in certain areas of their life, and so forth.

Tighten your seat belt. You are in for a great ride at the expense of my life unfolding in these pages. Let us begin our conversations, turn the page now.

Disclaimer

This book will have misspelled words that were used during childhood and young adulthood to add authenticity and depict the culture in which one was raised. I hope my life experiences and lessons learn will have a healing affect on people's lives. I am a private person, but I desire to save others from pain and a waste of valuable time in arenas they are not familiar with.

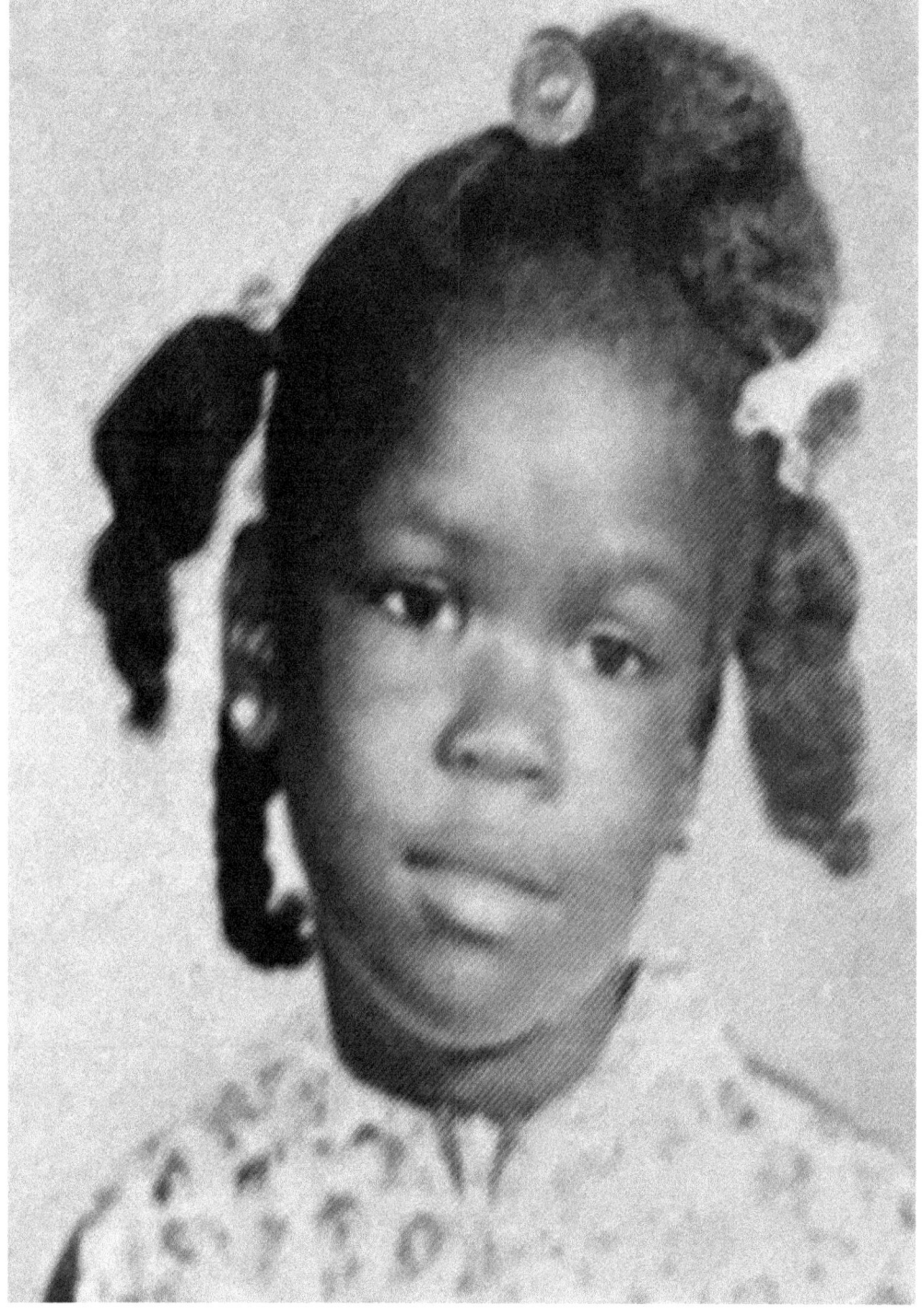

Happy Beginnings

THE HAPPIEST DAYS of my life were in early childhood. Back in the day, you had to be in the house before the streetlights came on. If you happened not to make it in the house before the streetlights came on, you felt a dark heavy cloud of fear and doom. Seriously you thought you might not make it to live through the evening. Parents back then had their method of raising kids. They put the fear of themselves in your heart. You did not stay in a room when grown folks were talking, and you dare not interrupt their conversations even if you politely said excuse me. You better have a good reason for interrupting them, such as the house is about to burn down; grandma is having an asthma attack/ heart attack. You get the picture. In those days, the neighbor helped raise kids. If a child happens to be discovered by Ms. Tiny doing something you did not have any business doing, and if it warrants a whipping, then Ms. Tiny whips you. That was the neighborhood law. Whoever caught you in the act administers the whipping, and if you were lucky, they would advocate that your parents and or grandparents not whip you anymore. Yes, you were liable to get two to three whippings in one day. That was enough to fix your mind not to ever do that act again. During those days, Children stayed within their fenced yards. Your siblings were your playmates. It was very seldom that me and my brother were allowed to play with other children in the neighborhood. If you did get to play with others, it was soon cut short for some made-up reason to send the playmate home. Christmas and a couple of days after Christmas, you were allowed to play in the streets with all neighborhood children. There were those steel skates that fastened to whatever shoes you had on. You had to use a key to tighten up the steel skates to your feet. The smaller kids were pulled in a nice big red wagon by all the older children whether they wanted to or not. All the caretakers sat on their porch watching the kids. Once again, whoever caught you doing anything wrong was the one to administer a whipping and then take you home to inform your parents or grandparents. In those days, you could sleep with windows heisted up in a one-story house without fear of anything happening.

By now, you have a little picture of what my childhood was. I want to focus on memorable events in my life that grow me in knowledge, experience, and strength. I remember falling asleep in a big white shaggy rug like a chair during a summer day. I remember God taking me on a spiritual journey. I was around the age of five to six years old. I know that he showed me my whole life but told me when I awoke; I would not remember anything he had shown me. He said I would only remember the thought He had shown me what my life would be. Before I awaken, I asked God why I cannot keep the memory. He did not give me an explanation. I awaken to my God-sister tapping me on my toe lightly. She wanted me to wake up to keep her company. She and her mother had to move in with me, my brother Rodney, and our maternal grandparents.

As a little girl, God was my imaginary best friend. Unlike kids that speak aloud to their imaginary best friends, I did not. I talked to God in my heart and mind regularly. I was in a wonderful time of purity and innocence in my life living with my grandparents. I was remarkably close to my grandfather R.C. Artis. My grandfather was a very tall, bright skin, handsome Black man. His mother was a full-blooded Cherokee Indian. Her name was Beulah, and she lived on an Indian reservation somewhere in Alabama. My grandfather ran away from home when he was a young boy due to his father's severe beatings.

My grandmother was as Black as tar, a full-figured woman that wore Black trimmed glasses. She, too, ran away from home when she was young due to severe beatings from one of her parents. My mother got pregnant in her last year of school with me. When I was born, my grandfather fell hard in love with me, so he took me from my mother while she was still in the hospital. My grandfather told my biological mother, "This is my baby now."

I was "granddaddy's" baby for years, and he invested as much valuable time with me as he could. My brother Rodney was my grandmother's favorite. He could not go to sleep without her being in bed with him or her laying a dress that she had worn on the bed before he would go to sleep. My brother was a chubby, adorable light skin boy. He loved to eat. He was a bit slow when it came to certain things. I felt love, comfort, and protection living with my grandparents. There was never a lack of food, clothes, or anything. Our lights were never turned off. There was always heating, blankets, and all other items that provided one comfort.

I recall going with granddaddy on one of his going out evenings. We lived on Evergreen Street on the East side of town. Down the road from our house was Browns community store, around the corner, and down the street from the fresh fish market off 21st street. I had to paint a picture first of the neighborhood. It was a neighbor friendly, mind your own business unless invited, convenient amenities neighborhood. I loved my neighborhood and my grandparents. I stayed home alone playing by myself. My granddaddy got tired of me sitting alone and playing alone while

Rodney followed grandmother foot to foot. He told my grandmother that he was taking me with him, and that was it. "This is my grandbaby, and I am taking her with me, and ain't a damn thing is going to happen to her." He said, "I will kill a nagger about my grandbaby. Grandmother could not say anything else but let me go.

There is a small dirt road off Evergreen Street that leads to a house back up in the woods. The place was called "Big Mama's House." Big Mama was a beautiful full-figure Black woman entrepreneur. She sold liquor, moonshine, buck, and white lightning. These homemade liquor drinks were made with different ingrediencies and could be called by different names depending on where one was from. Big Mama's house was within reasonable walking distance from our home. When we arrived, Big Mama had been expecting my grandfather. We walked through the living room, where men were sitting, talking, and drinking their liquor and smoking cigarettes.

Granddaddy and I sat in the kitchen with big mama herself. Granddaddy often visited her house on payday Fridays after work to unwind. Granddaddy sat me on a red milk carton that he placed on top of big mama's Kitchen table. He sat his pistol between my two feet and told me that the gun was loaded and careful not to kick or hit the gun. I nodded my head to say ok. Granddaddy went on to drink with big mama. They sat there and talked about what was going on in the world, "who got stabbed," shot, killed, and or who "got caught sleeping with someone else in the neighborhood." Back in my day, they did not call where you lived the Hood. They called it by its street's name and the neighborhood we lived in were nice houses of all shapes and styles. While granddad and big mama sometimes talked, guys who were drinking in the living room would yell out profanity toward one another. The famous saying was: "you are a damn lie" or "kiss my ass." Big mama, half-drunk herself, would say, stop all that cursing; we have a baby here. They would stop for a moment, and sooner than later, they were back at it, cursing and threatening one another. Big mama would say again did not I tell you, Mother Fu___; we have a child in here to keep down all that damn cursing."

As the evening got later, I would look at those men in the living room. Their whole facial looks & clothing would change as they got drunk. People would not even look like themselves as they were sloppy drunk. As witness this, I said to myself as a little girl, "If drinking makes you look like that, I never want to drink." As a result, I took my first drink when I was in my early twenties, and with that first drink, I was deafly afraid of becoming an alcoholic like my grandfather and uncles. My grandfather was what people might call a functional drunk. When he was not drinking, he was hard to be around. He was very cranky and short with others, but not me.

When granddaddy was ready to go home after drinking, he said, "Come on, little black heifer," we got to go. He picked me up off the red milk carton and sat me on my feet on the floor. We began our trip walking down the dirt road toward Evergreen Street. I felt special; I went with my grandfather into his world. He protected me. He made sure I ate and had soda pop to drink. As we walked down the dirt road, granddaddy stopped and looked at me. He started to laugh and say, "Who bought you boots? You look like pencils in a book sack." Granddaddy then got a little serious and said, here is some hush mouth money. This was not my last time going to big mama's house or getting hush mouth money. After a couple of times he gives me money, I started pondering. What is hush mouth money? My mind was perplexed. I wanted to know what hush mouth money was. I asked God. Remember, God was my imaginary friend. God, what is hush mouth money? The answer came to me just as clear as a bell: granddaddy do not want you to tell him. I chuckled quietly to myself. Why I would tell on the love of my life. In those days, "children are seen and not heard," so I never told granddaddy that he had nothing to worry about and that he did not need to give me hush mouth money because I would never tell anyone. What is so funny about that is that I did not see where he was doing anything wrong; he just got drunk with big mama. LoL! The innocence I had. Wow!

After going to big mama's house on occasions with granddaddy. I began to be troubled. Granddaddy would always start his sentence with "little black heifer." "Little black heifer do not be like your mother. Get your education; "do not depend on a man to do a damn thing for you." Do you hear me, little black heifer? I would say yes, sir. I began to think that my skin tone was ugly. For a brief time, I wished I were granddaddy's skin tone: light skin. If granddaddy did not have kinky black hair, he could pass as a white man. These thoughts were short-lived thanks to God. Finally, on one of our walks from big mamas, I asked God why he calls me this. Does he feel sorry for me? An answer came quickly: "Little Black Heifer" is his affectionate name for you because he loves your skin tone, and you are little thing. I received total peace with his nickname for me but only he could call me that. I never thought of wanting to be light skin anymore. Some of you may still not understand the nick name and imagine it as derogatory. I do not. It is the tone and pitch of how my grandfather called me "Little Black Heifer," joking and loving tone. My grandfather's parents lived during the time of picking cotton, and the slavery mentality was very much still in the mindset of Black people. Remember, my grandfather ran away when he was a young boy due to cruel beatings he suffered from by his father. My great grandfather was doing what was done to him by his father, which may have been during slavery or close to it. Old habits or generational habits are sometimes hard to break.

Later, when I got a little older, I found out that my grandfather was "a ladies' man," and that big mama was one of the women he was allegedly dating. I accompanied my grandfather to his women's homes. My grandfather told me that he had been poisoned twice by women and that he did not eat from a woman unless he watched the women cook the meal and he gets the first plate. I remember granddaddy would not even eat my cooking when I came of age. Some experiences in life lock your mind into protective habits that one does not break.

I remember a time when I went to visit one of my grandfather's girlfriends. This lady had children. My grandfather and I were going to sleep overnight with this family. My grandfather gently rehearsed me if I was questioned where we had been what to say. I said, ok, granddaddy, I got it. The lady told my grandfather that I could take a bath with her daughter. My grandfather was hesitant, but she convinced him that we both were girls and had the same thing. The lady's daughter and I went to the bathroom to bathe. I was happy to have someone other than my brother to talk and play. We both got into the tub. The young lady began to make sexual advances on me. I did not fear it because my protector was right outside the bathroom door, sitting in the living room. The young lady began to place her hairy vagina on my shoulder. I turned to look, and it scared the Hell out of me. I turned around quickly, not to show fear. I said to myself, "This girl and I do not have the same thing." Lol! I do not have hair on mine. I had to shake my mind into thinking straight. I felt that the young lady did it by mistake, so I did not say anything. The young lady asked me, "Have I ever done it. I asked her, "done what?" She said, "had sex." I quickly told the young lady no, and I did not want to. She then placed herself on my shoulder again. I told her that she better stop, or I am going to tell my granddaddy. The girl did it again. I told her that I would scream for my granddaddy if she did not stop. She did it again. Right at that moment, I screamed! "Granddaddy! Granddaddy! Granddaddy! My protector, my knight in shining armor, came busting through the bathroom door to rescue me. He immediately threw a towel around me, scared himself, not knowing what was wrong. He kept saying, "What is wrong with you? He tried looking me over to see if I had any cuts, bruises, marks, but I would not let him. I was in a major Grammy award acting role! Lol! I was falling all to the floor, crying says, "Granddaddy, Granddaddy, Oh Granddaddy." He got even more upset and angry. He asked what was wrong with granddaddy's baby. Oh, this actor knew it was time for the major line: "Granddaddy she, she, and she." Granddaddy said, "she what?" The actor in me knew I could not stall too long. I went on to say, "Granddaddy, she tried to get me. She put her cat on me." That was all it took. He did not ask any more questions. The Cherokee Indian came out like a raging bull. Granddaddy then began to pick up my clothes and told me to hurry up and to get dressed. He left me in the bathroom alone to get dressed. I could hear my grandfather outside of the door cursing and threatening the lady and her daughter. One of the statements I heard him say was, "nobody messes with that little Black gal, my grandbaby. I ought to shoot this MF up, you and your bull "dagging" ass daughter." The drama queen (me) was incredibly pleased with this comment. I did not want granddaddy to get too mad and make good on his threats, so little drama queen (me) dressed like superman in a phone booth. I came out of the bathroom crying like a baby to draw his attention to take me out of the lady's home quickly and to keep him out of trouble.

Gifting

HUMANS ARE BORN with instincts just like animals. During this time of my innocence, I had a deep-down confident feeling that my grandfather would always protect me from all hurt, harm, and danger. He would always defend my honor, even if I had lied. I cannot imagine any child, woman or man never experience this type of security at a time in their life, however brief it may have been.

I pray for you all that have never experience this type of security: Father, God in the precious name of your son Jesus Christ. I ask for my passion for loving people and wrapping the person reading these lines in your secure love and protection. My gentle savior, I ask that this person especially feel your presence, whether a gentle breeze flow on them, they feel a warm blanket of heat flow from the top of their head to the bottom of their feet, they began to laugh or cry with joy. Let the dam break the doors of their hurt to bring cleansing to their body, mind, and spirit. My love and creator, however, you choose to bless them. Please do it, Lord, God. I ask you God, when they began to feel insecurities, which are overwhelming in their hearts, minds, and spirits say not so, I know that God loves me and that feeling immediately goes away swiftly in your son name's Jesus Christ. Amen!

As a little girl between the ages of four to six years old, I began to have dreams. I did not understand why I had usual dreams. Maybe because my imaginary friend, God, wanted to talk back to me in dreams. The dreams were about things to come. We all dream dreams from time to time, whether we are children, young adults, or senior adults. My dreams were different because they were trance-like realities. I felt like I was there inside the dreams. The dreams were so surreal. In the dreams, I would witness the events around a family member's death. After my first dream like this, I would pray so hard to protect that specific family member. I would talk to my imaginary friend, God. Please do not allow this to happen. I was only around four or five years old and had these types of dreams. I lacked understanding of life, but I believed in what I saw in dreams. My imaginary friend, God was as real as you and me even though I could not see Him. I just knew he was real, and He had power. One might think I got the Ideal of God from through the church. I do not remember going to church with anyone, not even my grandparents. My grandmother did not attend church due to being used and abuse in church. My grandfather did not dot the door of a church. Thus, I had no memory at all of church. My grandmother was a tranquil woman. She never sat down and talked to me or my brother about prayer, bible scriptures, church, God, or anything related to this area. Wow! God bless the child who has his own or, should I say, come into his or her meaning of life. My dreams would happen every so often when it was time for a family member to leave this world/pass away. As this gift kept occurring, I began to gain an understanding of that gift, and I became confident in it. After a few dreams came true, I was confident that whenever someone in the family was to pass away. As a child, I never shared this gift with anyone. As mentioned before, raising children in that time that "children were seen and not heard." Children did not have personal rights, space, or freedom of speech. Plus, I did not want people to think I was crazy. Being this young and sheltered, I had the idea that crazy people would put you in a padded room in a strait jacket. I learn early in life; you do not share everything you experience in life with people because one does not want to risk getting locked up in seeing things that normal people do not see or experience.

Great Change

THE LAST DREAM of seeing the person's face that would pass away was my grandfather, my heart. I was almost twelve years old and resided with my biological mother since my grandmother died in 1974. I cried for days into weeks. I prayed until I would pass out from deep prayer to God to spare my love, my protector, my grandfather's life. I prayed for my grandfather for long periods of time because I knew he loved me unconditionally, and no matter what I did in life, his love would not die for me. This man talked strength into me every time he spent time with me or saw me. It may sound strange to you reading this book, but he would say, "Little Black Heifer, don't be like your mother, get your education, don't depend on a man to do a damn thing for you." My grandfather told me this every time he saw me for years, whether sober or dead drunk. He would tell me what to look out for in life when dealing with people. On the day of my grandfather's death, I felt an urgent need to see him right when he got off work. I begged my mother to let me go to his job right when he got off work, but she would not allow me, stating, "Daddy told me to stop sending you to his job." I began to cry. During my puberty years, I never cried unless I received carpal punishment. I was tough. I was the oldest of six young siblings. My mother would not allow me to go to my grandfather's job. I went back upstairs of our home feeling like dread, waiting to hear the news, or God will not allow death to take my heart away, my grandfather. I just knew I would convince my mother to let me go because she sent me every Friday to get money from him. She would tell me to tell grandfather that I needed money for various things, knowing he would not deny me, his little Black heifer. Yes, he was still calling me this at eleven years old. I sat in the room that I shared with siblings, alone, and stuck. I prayed and waited. The news came about an hour later that my grandfather had died.

My love, my protector, and my grandfather was gone. I had no one now that I could depend on, much less feel safe around. I intuitively knew that I would catch Hell from then on because I had no one else that loved and protected me the way my grandfather did. He died walking out of a storefront house, stepping down while drinking a fifth of MD 20/20. My heart ached for days, months, and years afterward. It was times that I feared that I would forget what he looked like as time passed. But constant prayer for years eventually healed this profound loss in my life. The old folks say you will understand it by and by, and I did.

If only I could have made it to his job? When I arrived at his job site in the past, he would postpone getting him a drink. He would ensure I had what I needed and was safely home. Sometimes he would not even drink. He had gotten hip to my mother, sending me to his job asking for money for me when it was for cigarettes, or other household needs. Grandfather began to keep me with him on the weekend and ensured I spent money on everything my heart desired. He would take me over to the Brown's neighborhood store. The store had fresh lunch meat in bread shaped logs, which the meat cutter had to slice individual pieces. The store had all that hard-to-find odd old food that older people enjoyed. Youngsters like spiced ham and bologna. He would purchase items to cook for him and me over the weekend.

My grandfather had a great disappointment in my mother for the lifestyle she chose to live. The type of men that she dated and or married. The men my mother married were either drug addicts or drug dealers. I must be forthcoming. My mother eluted to my grandfather not being who I thought he was, and she would ask me if he had touched me in the wrong areas. I would get angry with her and say, "No, my grandfather would never do that to me." She would make underlining comments over the years but never come out confessing anything. My mother did tell me that her brother raped her in a sugar cane field. This uncle was older and never lived in the home with my grandparents. He was a child from a previous marriage of my maternal grandmother. My mother warned me of him if ever I would contact him, never be alone with him and if so, watch him. I had never seen this man but in pictures and my grandmother's funeral. I took great heed to my mother in this area. I visited my uncle as a young adult woman out of curiosity. As a young adult woman, I saw what mother meant. My uncle, lust after me by looking at me with the eyes of a man wanting a woman, trying to play it off with jokes and stories about what happened in the past. It gave me the creeps! I got out of his home as soon as possible to avoid him attacking me.

Memories

THE INCIDENT I had with my biological uncle reminded me of an event a beloved aunt shared with me near the end of her life. My Aunt Verdi was born in 1912; she was a great beauty in her time. From time to time, older people in our family would out of know where mention, "You should have seen your aunt Verdi in her younger years. She was a gorgeous, shapely woman." When these people described my aunt, it reminded me of someone giving a description of a lovely Queen. The conviction and emotions these people displayed during their description of my aunt were touching. After a third family member acted this way to describe my aunt, I pay attention to how they look and act while mentioning her beauty and shape.

The Lord, God Almighty, moved me to start visiting my aunt in her nursing home. The Lord had changed his way of dealing with me about future passing away of a loved one. It was a great urgency that made me feel that I had to see her and keep seeing her until this spirit of urgency lifted. I admit I had never gone to see her in the nursing home. My aunt was placed in a nursing home after her adopted daughter could no longer care for her at home. Verdi had developed alhazmiers. She was a great danger to herself and her family. I remember one incident that happened before she went into a nursing home. In my youth, and due to the environment, I grew up in after leaving my grandparents' house, I slept with weapons near me.

I always slept with a huge butcher knife under my mattress. My aunt Verdi, searching around my room, found my butcher's knife. She had sectioned off a part of the house and would not allow anyone to come in. She would open the living room door waving the huge butcher knife, stating she "will kill a son of a bitch if they try to go at her." "Wow." Everyone was wondering how did she got such a big sharp knife? I had to tell everyone that it was mine and that I kept it under my mattress. A brief time after that and other incidents of violence my beloved aunt displayed, my cousin, her adopted daughter, had to make the unwanted decision to place her in the nursing home. My cousin cried for several nights about putting the mom she knew in a nursing home. She did not want to place her in the nursing home. My aunt Verdi had been the strong pillar in the family. Aunt Verdi was the one person everyone ran to when they were in trouble and needed her connections.

My first trip to visit my aunt in the nursing home was good. Remember God gave me a gift for understanding and ministering to all social classes and circumstances. I have learned to watch and observe people and their environment to avoid difficult outcomes or, should I say, adverse reactions. Verdi knew who I was and was happy to see me. As soon as I sat down, she jumped in conversation about her adopted daughter, her deceased sister daughter. She asked me when the last time I saw her daughter and asked me to tell her to come to see her. I told her I would. After a couple of visits, Verdi then began to use what she thought would get her daughter to come to see her, money. She would tell me, tell mama (nickname for her daughter), that she has some money for her and that she needs to come to get it. The nursing home receives all Verdi's funds for caring for her, so she did not have any extra money to give her daughter.

Upon the fourth visit with my aunt, I was curious. I prayed for how I would ask her the question that had been burning in my head. I was in deep prayer during my questioning. I ask her, "Verdi, why didn't you have any children of your own? You helped raise so many of us coming up?" Verdi's response was, "I couldn't have any." I prayerfully and gentle asked her again, "why?" I was not prepared for what came next. Verdi said, "Well, my male brothers and cousins gang raped me. I fought back with all that I had. They ended up breaking my back in three "different places," they messed up my insides, and the doctors told me that I would never walk again nor have children. "I was in bed for a year before I learned how to walk again." I was shocked by her response. I said OK and quickly moved to a happy event by asking her when the church people were coming out again. She glowed with excitement when I asked her about the church people as she refers to them. She began to sing her favorite song, "Glory, Glory, alleluia since I laid my burdens down, Glory, Glory, alleluia since I laid my burdens down, friends don't treat me like they used to, since I laid my burdens down." I began to sing with her, and my spirit was perplexed by the devastating event she shared with me about her life. "Wow." That explains what I did not understand growing up being baby sat by my aunt.

I thought she could be crazy at times, and sometimes I thought, "What could have happened in her life to cause her to be the way she was. She would chain up doors. She would keep certain areas under lock and key and constantly checked the rooms to ensure no one had broken in. She would also tell me details and sometimes vague imagery of what she experienced as a grown woman after the first brutal event in her life.

For instance, one time, Verdi and I were in the bathroom. She was cleaning the tube as best as she could. My aunt began to talk to me about a relationship with a man. She said she remembers dating this man on the side. My aunt lived with her husband but had a boyfriend as well. The boyfriend offered her something to drink. She told her boyfriend she did not want anything to drink three times. He insisted that she must be thirsty, and he wanted her to be comfortable. He told her, please let me get you something to drink. Verdi agreed to a glass of water. The man left Verdi alone in the room. Verdi sneaked out of the room and watched him from a distance as he fixed the glass of water. Verdi said she saw the man put a powder-like substance in her water. He brought the glass of water back to her and offered it to her. Verdi thanked him and placed water on the dresser by the bed. She said she began to make short talk, and soon she created a way to leave right away by telling a lie. My aunt then began to tell me, "When a man wants to get the milk out of him, he'll do anything to get it out of him." As a little girl, I did not know what she was talking about. I did not ask my aunt any question because it was instilled in me that "A child should be seen and not heard." In other words, you do not engage in grown folk conversation, and you do not question adults. I asked my close friend," God, what is milk that a man has to get out of him." God never answered that question. I wondered about that for years to come. I knew it was valuable information. I soon gave up understanding and thought to myself, one day I will understand what she said. I had great hope as a child that the information Verdi shared would come in handy one day. As a little girl, I enjoyed older people. They had so much wisdom and knowledge about life. I found them to be so exciting and entertaining. I loved hearing about how they grew up and how they did things. I would rather sit and spend time with my elderly than young people my age. I always wanted to learn how to live and valuable life, to avoid: bad situations and destructive relationships.

    Later in my adult life, I began to seek the truth about why individual family members lived and carried themselves a certain way. My aunt's and mom's testimonies are just two events that I found intriguing. My uncle was another interesting character. One of my uncles was the perfect likeness to his mother. My grandmother was dark as night, full-figured Black women. My uncle was a stocking well build dark as night black man with his mother's features. My uncle was always in a foul mood. He was a grumpy, mean-spirited, and very cynical person. Whenever I went to see him, I was so glad to see him, but he would always curse me out and say, "I do not have any money, Tonya. When I was growing up, I had no one to help me. I would lean on my uncle for help growing up and going through college. When I became an adult, I did not need his support anymore, but he still thought that the only reason I came to see him was for money. I would tell my uncle I am an adult now and I do not need your money. He then said, "Well give me some money." I would tell him, Uncle, if I had it I would. My uncle's negative, nasty disposition made me curious. I pondered now and then on what happened to him in his life for him to be the way he was. I prayed a prayer of God revealing the secrets of family member's past and reasons for the way they act. I thought it was important to know what is in my family's bloodline and history.

One Thanksgiving holiday, while I was in my mid-thirties, I went to talk to my aunt, my uncle's wife, but she was not there. My uncle greeted me as usual, "Hey Tonya, I ain't got no money." I told my uncle I did not come for money and why do you always say that? He said, "You don't come around unless you want money." I told my uncle that I had no one growing up and I needed the support when I was young, and God bless you to help me. I asked my uncle where my auntie was, he said with her people. I told him that she knew I was coming, that I needed to talk to her about something. He called her up on her cell phone and said that I was there waiting for her. We sat at his kitchen table. He offered me a cup of coffee. It was a chilly night, and I had just got into drinking coffee. I said yes to the offer. My uncle makes the best coffee. We sat at the table sipping on our coffees.

Out of nowhere, my uncle began talking about his childhood and young adulthood. I was quiet and tentative with every word that came out of his mouth. He started by telling me, "You know your grandmother had favoritism to her light skinned children. He went on to say, "I was the 'black sheep' of the family." "My mother told me that I was never going to amount to nothing and that I would end up dead in the gutter." Wow! That blew my mind, but I kept quiet as he told me more. He told me that he and my mother had been remarkably close for a period. They looked out for one another. My uncle was older than my mother. He was my mother's protector. I told my uncle that it was funny because my mother said my grandmother had favoritism towards boys and did not want a girl. I went on to tell my uncle that my mother said she was the "black sheep" of the family. He said no that he was. I kept quiet from there on by the anointing of God for answered my prayer. I wanted to know why he was so angry and hostile all the time about everything, so now I know.

You know, I overheard someone say the same thing about me when I was a troubled teen. The Person said that I was the Black sheep of the family. I came to stay with my adult cousin when I was fourteen years old. Her adopted father, who loved her dearly, would talk about me late at night with her husband. For days and months, my cousin's adopted father said that I was no good and that I was always getting into trouble, that I would graduate from the jailhouse, that I was not going to amount to anything. A pastor I know from an adult past use to say, "just because someone calls you something does not mean it is true. You can be whatever you set out to be." As a child, when I started living with my biological mother, she would call me a dummy because I could not focus on school, and I was in ESE classes. For a long time, I thought I was dumb. I thought about going into the military. I would see the world and have a better life than I had living with my biological mother. I started living with my biological mother around six years old and after my grandmother passed. I lived with my biological mother through two separate husbands. One husband was a great father but was unfaithful to his marriage. The second husband was physically abusive and a drug addict. He used needle to shot drugs in his veins. I had to constantly watch out for used needles to avoid me and my small siblings stepping on. My mother had three children from her second husband. By this time, there were six children, including myself. As a pre-teen I had to cook, clean and wash everyone's clothes in the house. My drug addict stepfather and mother had a grocery basket filled of dirty clothes I had to push a couple of blocks to the laundry mat and wash Gods had his "hands on my life" for a long time.

Getting back to overhearing relatives talk about me, after hearing the words my cousin's father said when I was in my teens ("That girl ain't going to be nothing, she is going to graduate from the jail house. She ain't nothing but trouble"), something came upon me and said I will be somebody. I accepted that revelation and believed it even though my situation was grave looking. I did not know when my cousin's father and her husband were going to plot to get me thrown out of the house from one day to the next. Funny, although my cousin's father talked about me frequently when he thought I was not listening, I enjoyed being around him. He was old and full of wisdom. I used to sit with him and play Pokeno. He told me about his past and the things he did. He told me about various healing herbs and how people made certain things to live. He told me he was very handsome, and the women loved him. He told me that he had a woman for every day of the week and clothes at their houses. He told me about various relationships he was tangled up in. One time there two women that were friends and lived next door to each other. He was having sex with both, and they suspected him of doing so. Still later in life, in his old age, he had three women with whom he was sexually active. One was a woman in her mid-thirties, other women was in her mid-twenties who loved being around older people like me, and last one allegedly his relative by marriage. So as one can see, my life was unstable emotionally and physically. I lived with these relatives from fourteen to young adulthood in college in a rooming house. The rooming house was full of diverse types of people, including drug addicts. There was Knocks at the front all times of night from roomers coming and going.

Mind

THE BLACK FAMILIES around my time of growing up were complex households.

The parents, older adults grew up hard, and they raised their children the same way. There is nothing wrong with a few hard methods they used, but the ones that took children down mentally and emotionally are not what God intended. Every Child is different and require different methods of child rearing. Some would say, why then does God allow these things to happen to the innocent. It goes back to the Garden of Eden when Adam and Eve disobeyed God (Genesis 3:1-5). That is when the knowledge of good and evil was conceived in man's heart. So, the generations after Adam and Eve, two spirits are wrestling inside of everyone: one good and one evil. It depends on which spirit wins during specific situations. Your spiritual being willing to do good every time, but your flesh wants gratification. Thus, even being believers, we may struggle at times with doing the right things.

As a teenager, I had low self-esteem. Nicknames are not always suitable for children depending on the name. My mother used to call me a string bean, bean pole, and dummy. These were the names she called me, thinking it was funny because she often laughed at my sad continence or irritated looks. The bible said, "As a man thinketh so is he" (Proverbs 23:7). If a person is called something long enough, they may be subject to believe it. I thought I was dumb for years up until my late years in my adulthood. I was not too fond of my body features. My mother uses to say that I was "shaped like a white girl, pancake booty." My legs were long and skinny. It appeared that the only thing I had going for myself: my facial beauty, good hair as our Black culture refers, and breasts. I had to pray as a young girl not to give me big breasts because that ran in our family and cause significant discomfort to women in our family. Bras were costly for most women in our family. It is worth mentioning from a young, innocent child into late adulthood, I was attracted to well-groomed, nice-looking men but thought the act of sex was disgusting: the sweating, the fluids, Yuck!

As mentioned in the previous paragraph, I was quiet and standoffish as a teenager suffering from low self-esteem. I harbored anger. I would fight at the drop of a hat. I was not the arguing type—if there was a reason I had to fight; I just fought. I did not believe in making negative comments and threatening the person that wanted to fight me. I would make a statement to ensure that the person who wanted to fight me. I would tell them that I did not want to fight, but I would if pushed, I would. Funny, I can remember my first fight. My brother and I were walking home from school. We were in elementary school for the first time. I was tall, and my brother was handsome, short, and round. This little girl jumped out of nowhere and told us that we could not pass on her sidewalk. We passed anyway, and that little girl who was smaller than both my brother and me beat us down, and we did not raise a figure to do anything because we were taught for years before we went to school we had better not ever fight. My chubby brother ran and left me getting beat. When I got home, my grandmother spanked me and asked me why I allowed the girl to beat my brother and me. I told her that she said to us that we better not ever fight. She said, "Yes, I told you that, but I never told you to get your brains knocked out of you. "You better go to school tomorrow and if that little girl starts with you all again? You better beat the hell out of her, and I mean that."

Why did grandmother tell me that!!!! I have been fighting since that incident. Living with my biological mother was a war zone. I escaped when I was fourteen years old from Miami, Florida, to Jacksonville, Florida. I had seen so much violence, sexual abuse, and drugs that I was full of fury, un-forgiveness, and bitterness. I had made up my mind that no one was going to get the best of me. I was not going "to be got" in relationships, no matter what kind. When I got to be a teenager, I felt I could stand up against any abusive situations that I was not able to when I was a child.

Experiences

I WAS ELEVEN years old, When I was molested by an older male cousin of a beloved aunt by marriage. He was light-skinned and very handsome, but my mind was not on sex, kissing, or anything else a grown man expects from a woman. I was proud to have a good-looking cousin. He was his mother's favorite. For years, my preference were dark skin Black men. When I got older, any well-groomed attractive man with a little swagger was of interest to me. Let us continue. My aunt would get into arguments with her husband, trying to protect her favorite son. He would be disrespectful to her husband at times and remind him that he was not his father. My mother married this beloved aunt's brother. My stepfather was the last to be born, and all his older siblings were females. My mother would ask my aunt by marriage to babysit us over knight at times. My brother Rodney and I would share a bed. It was hard to fall asleep in someone else's house when one was not used to sleeping overnight outside of home. Rodney was still chubby little boy but did not take- up too much room in the twin-size bed.

    One night, my older cousin came into the bedroom while pitch black and began to slide his hands my PJ pants to my virginal area. He played with my private parts. I could not move because I was scared and could not believe what was happening. I was too embarrassed to do or say anything. I thought about telling my mother, but an internal instinct kicked in: if I told my mother, as weak-minded as she is for this man, she would do nothing, and I would be called a "fast tail" lying little girl. I also did not want to lose the sweetest love of my abuser's mother. I had not experienced this type of love sense my maternal grandfather died. I was in a tricky situation in my child's mindset at that time.

From that time on, I would beg my mother not to leave me at my beloved aunt's house to stay overnight. I would try to think up ways to keep staying overnight. My excuses never worked. I even reminded her that grandmother never allowed us to stay overnight with anyone. I asked her why she was breaking her own personal rule of letting us stay with someone. She said they had business to deal with and were not able to take us with her. I told my mother that I was old enough to keep my siblings so that we could stay in our own home, and she would not have to travel to pick us up. We will be home. That did not work. After that first molestation experience, I would try to stay awake at night so that my grown cousin would not violate me. I would pinch my brother for as long as I could to keep him from going to sleep so I would not get sexually fondled. I felt sorry about pinching my brother to keep him awake, but I needed help. I could only do so much for so long before I fell asleep. My grown man cousin came in and violated me when he thought I was sleep; I did not care how late it got. He waited until all was still in the am hours and did what he thought I did not feel.

I would stay still and function as though I was asleep because I was so shame and embarrassed of what was going on. I was confused and hurt by my closest friend, God. I asked Him why he allowed this to happen to me. Why? I was a good-hearted person. God never answered. I then began to change my way of communicating with God. I prayed that he would bury the memory of the molestations that I experience at my male-grown cousin's hand until I was old enough to manage it. I prayed for days, nights, months, and years. It took about three to four years for that memory to disappear for a season. God granted my prayer on that.

The memory did not re-surface until my fourteen-year-old teen sisters were sexually abused. My mother's husband at that time was having full intercourse with my sisters. My mother ignored my sisters when they told her what was going on. Our mother called them fast; and that they flop their bottoms around all the time. My mother did not take my sisters to be examined until the news got out in the neighborhood. I assume my mother feared going to jail for not doing anything about it. The sexual exploitation that my twin sisters experienced proves that when I was molested, my mother would not have done anything about what happened to me. If I had told my aunt about her son, she would not have done anything but call me a liar. In adulthood, another female cousin said that this same aunt's son tried to take advantage of her, and she ran and told. My beloved aunt called her a "fast tail girl," and a liar, and that her son did not do this. The two sisters did not talk for about a year because of this incident.

Suicidal thoughts accompanied the low self-esteem that I had. I would say my low self-esteem started after residing for two years with my biological mother. Before then, I lived with my maternal grandparents, and life was great, safe, peaceful, fun, and enjoyable. My grandmother was my mother, and my mother was my big sister. I did know that my big sister was my biological mother from the beginning, which was not hidden from me. I was a happy child during the years I resided with my grandparents. I developed low self-esteem and suicidal tendencies living with my biological mother. I still had my imaginary friend "God." I would beg God to end my life so I could come live with him in heaven, life on earth was not for me. After a year of requesting God to take my life and no results, I began to think of ways to end my life. My plans involved having the money to buy items to take my own life and finding the resources that would be a swift and speedy death. I had these thoughts and planned to take my life up until my early adulthood life. My last battle with suicidal thoughts was upon my first marriage, in my early thirties to mid-thirties. I had married a man that I thought my family had approved of, only to come to find out that all they wanted was for me to be with him to use him for his money and resources. They talked me into dating him, which was not hard to do because I was attracted to him. My family never intended on me marrying this man. When they found out, they were all angry and upset. I was confused. I was a new believer in Jesus Christ, the Father, and the Holy Ghost.

Let us go back to the beginning my dating this man before marriage. I had just given my life over to Christ, and I did not know much at all. I was a baby in the spiritual as well as the bible. From a worldly point of view, I was a mature and successful professional woman. I had the following under my belt: A four-year bachelor's degree graduate, An Assistant Program Coordinator at the Family visitation center. The family visitation center was where parents visit children, they no longer have custody or legal rights to see independently. I was a foster Care Counselor with the department of children and Families Services. I had been managing other adults for about two years before becoming born again. I worked in both positions. On my weekly primary job, I was a Foster Care Counselor and a Supervisor on my second full time job. I was tough like nails and believed my strength came from my grandfather. Getting back to my point, I was an infant in the things of God but an experienced leader and seasoned in the business environment.

Being a new believer, I was still doing quite a few things worldly. As the old Folks say: "the fish don't come out of the water gutted and cleaned." John 15:3 said, "The word cleanses the mind." I did not have time to read the bible. My time was consumed with the responsibility of leading people, and I had to be up on my game. I had a reputation for keeping up: being knowledgeable, dependable, and highly efficient. As a new believer, I was still sexing, drinking, dancing the reggae dance the butterfly, and cursing like a sailor. I felt so bad and tried so hard to stop cursing & swearing in my own strength. I felt self-condemnation for two years of trying to stop saying nasty stuff out of my mouth. I grew up in an atmosphere where grandfather cursed like a sailor, and all my uncles did too. Now I am in church, trying to learn how to live a positive, healthy lifestyle. My beloved aunt talked to me for years about giving my life to God. A next-door neighbor who gave me the creeps; a younger woman than I kept asking to go to church with her explained things to me in simple terms where I could understand the walk of a Christian, having a relationship with God. I would give her all kinds of excuses. If I come to God, I will be "right," not like those so-called Christians I see sneaking around sleeping with other men, wives, or women that look good to them and vice versa. It was nothing to see church folk in the hole in the wall nightclubs drinking in a corner and sometimes dancing on the floor. At times someone would put them on "Front Street and say, hey, deacon or pastor." They would be so drunk that they would speak back to the one that called them out. Every now and then, one that held such a position would make an excuse stating that God wants us to enjoy life. We can drink, Jesus drunk wine. As I grow in Christ later, I knew the difference. Before then, I knew nothing.

When I began to go to church with my next-door neighbor, I began to enjoy going even though I did not understand much. I figured that Church was a safe place, a hospital. I remember hearing older people say, "You'll understand by and by." For years, I hated that saying. After all, I was a woman of knowledge and wanted to know all I could know and learn. I got pregnant. I was hurt because I had just got saved and wanted to do things right, but I had strong urges that I could not control. I enjoyed having sex. I loved it. I loved being sexually explicit in my dancing. There were two things that I could not give up living for the Lord: sex and dirty dancing. I could give up drinking socially.

Unlike my grandfather, a functional alcoholic, I only drink from time to time. When I drank, I was scared as Hell that I was going to become an alcoholic and or a drug addict. These things were my family vices. I took my first drink around 23 to 24 years old, and I thought I would become an alcoholic. It scared me to death to have a substance alter your personality so that you end up becoming violent, locked up, for killing someone.

Getting back to the point I was trying to make. I got pregnant at the beginning of my new life in Christ Jesus. I wanted to be as good as I can. I did not want to become an alcoholic, fornicating drug-using Christians that I saw in the world. I knew I could not be perfect, but I wanted to live right, make a significant effort. You would think that was all. No, that was only part of my dilemma. Not only was I pregnant, but I did not know who the father was. You see, I slept with the husband-to-be and ex-finance within the same week I did not know what to do. Before I was born again, I was a regular woman, that thought like a man.

My grandfather was my only role model for learning about life. I juggled (3 to 4) men a week, all while working two full-time jobs. I still marvel at how I maintained. When I say, I thought like a man. I operated mentally as one. Physically I was very famine but calculating. So, I would mark my calendar of who I slept with, with their initials so if I ever "got caught up," I will know who the baby's father is. I practice safe sex, but condoms break, and birth control fail at times. I continued being sexually active, prior to marriage and being a newborn Christians. Your body muscles are used to being penetrated and the feelings of your sexual organs are not going to turn off. Old habits just do not go away overnight. The fish do not come out of the water/world gutted and clean. It is a process.

This sin almost cost me my life. I was in my second job, Assistant Program Coordinator at the family visitation center when I experienced severe pain in my abdominal area. I would pop two to three Motrin a day to make the pain go away. The pain kept coming back. I tried to hold out because I did not like taking pills because of family habits. I eventually popped Motrin all week. I had to work my day job through this pain as a Foster Care counselor. I have a high thresh-hold for pain. After going into the second week of pain and working hard, I scheduled a doctor's appointment. My primary doctor referred me to a specialist. The specialist examines me and then called another female physician in to verify what he saw. The doctor went outside the office to talk with the other doctor. I had enough time to get dressed. The specialist came back in to talk to me. He said that I was pregnant in the tubes and that he would not be going home that evening. I had this look on my face; my demeanor had changed from a professional to eastside hood look, mean mugging. I asked the doctor was he sure. He said yes, that is why I called for a second opinion. I told the doctor that I had to take my truck home, and I would come back. I needed time to think about this. I had never been sick to this extreme. I gave the doctor another eastside hood, mean mugging look. The doctor read my face, got in my face, and put his finger in my face, and said, if I allow you to walk outside my office and you drop dead, your family will be all over me, if I must? I will knock you out right here and now, so you will walk downstairs to the hospital. The doctor said I have already called downstairs they are waiting for you now. I slowly sat down after the doctor told me this and tried to think about what to do next. I called my supervisor at the department of children Family services and told her what was going on. Our relationship had always been professional. She knew I was a perfectionist. I was her manager in our second job. There was respect between her and me. She shifted into a panic mold as a woman with a grown child. I told her to calm down. She asked if anyone was there with me. I told her no; the doctor just gave me the news. She told me to tell the doctor to wait until she gets there. I told her that they could not wait. It is a life-and-death situation. I told her I would be all right. I had to call my babysitter and my mother. She said OK, but to call her when I could. I called my babysitter. She told me not to worry about my baby, my son. Quinton was only a toddler then. Now, the last call I dreaded making, my mother.

I talked with God. Lord, I am good, I am confident, that I know where I am going if I do not make it out of this surgery. My only concern was my son; God gives him someone that would take care of him as I have and will. Shield and protect him from all hurt and harm. Now, God, how do I break this news to my mother, who is still grieving over my middle brother's death from four months ago? My youngest brother is still in the hospital with brain trauma. Lord, I am her first-born child, her eldest.

Should I even call? Should I wait until I make it out of surgery? I began to talk to myself. What if I do not make it? How would my mother feel that she never heard my voice again and never got to say goodbye? I then decided to call my mother just in case. I called my mother. I said, "Hey, mom." She said with a frantic, dreaded tone, "what's wrong." I said nothing, "I was just calling." She said, "What's wrong." Well, mom, they are getting ready to have surgery on me. My mother began screaming and hollering, "Oh no, Lord not my first-born child." I tried to calm my mother down. I told her I was pregnant in the tubes, and they were about to burst. She finally calmed down enough to tell me, to tell the doctor to wait until she gets there. I told mom, mom they cannot wait, I must leave now to go to the emergency room, they must do surgery as soon as possible.

Walking through the Valley

I SQUEEZED IN, prior to her losing it, Mom, I love you, and I will talk to you later. I had to hang up and rush down to the emergency room of the hospital. It took me about five minutes to get to the hospital emergency room. The specialist office was part of the hospital, St. Vincent's hospital. When I arrived, an attendant asked me if I was Latonia Artis. I said yes. I was still downplaying the situation. I have a high thresh hold for pain, cannot be that bad. I completed paperwork. Again, I thought, it is not that serious. Before I could finish the paperwork, the nurse came in with a wheelchair and told me to get in, she was going to take me to my room. I popped into a chair. The nurse rushed me to my room. She told me to get undressed. So, I undressed as I normally would. I had to take off all my jewelry. I put on a hospital gown. The nurse immediately came back with an IV and the blood technician walked in with her. The nurse kept asking me where is your family. Are they on the way? My response to her was not yet, this was unexpected, and I just left my doctor's office. Both the nurse and the blood technician were sticking me with needles at the same time. The nurse was on my left side doing the IV and the blood technician was on my right side. Both ladies made comments, she is so calm. Little did they know that I was talking to God in my mind? After the nurse asked me for the fourth time where my family was, I remembered what a nurse told me when I had a complication with the pregnancy of my son. She said the key thing to remember is to always remain calm and stay focused. I kept this knowledge when it came to medical situations with anyone. I told God, Lord I need to know that you are here with me right now. Let me feel your presence. He answered. I felt as if someone had poured hot thick mud from the crown of my head to my face. I thanked God! Right after that, the nurse finally got the IV to go in. My veins are small, and they move so she was having a tough time finding a vein.

My family, my older cousin, was there when I came out of surgery. About two days later I was laying in the hospital bed thinking, God, you have not told me that this man is my husband, so I am going to stop seeing him and wait on who you have for me. Soon after that declaration, my church family members came to see me. When one of the Holy women walked to the other end of my bed, she got a swift revelation. She told me that God told her to tell me that my husband is on the way. She was so excited about the revelation that her body jumped and jerked prior to telling me. Me, still a baby in Christ, said within myself, so this man is my husband. This how I ended up marrying the man that in my ignorance of understanding was not to marry. God was going to send my husband after I said I was going to stop dating/sleeping with the man. This was a great spiritual lesson I learn later as my prophetic gifting increased: Never jump and speak what you see until you ask God how to deliver message. He may not want you to deliver all the details you see and or you need to wait until he gives instructions on how to break it down on that person's level of spiritual understanding in Christ. You can really delay or have a part in messing someone's life up. People can recover, and others may not recover. Prophecy can be a life and death situation. I never wanted this gift. When God revealed to me years ago what my gifting was, I was devastated. I told God, "No not that God, people do not like those people. They think you are seeing all their hidden places (nine times out of ten you are through the grace of the Holy Spirit) I do not want to be accountable for such a gift that will require me to live a certain lifestyle that I do not want too.

Sexual Appetite

BACK TO PLANNING to marry, All the way to the courthouse, something just did not feel right but I went on anyway because I thought I was just nervous or had cold feet. I felt weird. I was ready to settle down and wanted to have my own man not someone else or sharing a man. Three of the guys I dated at one time had other women and one of the three was married. I almost fail in love with the married man. When he told me he did not love me. My mind shifted into man mold. I immediately bedded him. Afterwards I cleaned myself up and invented an excuse to get him out of my house. Walked him to the door. While he was standing at the door smiling, I told him, it is over, do not call me or beep me and I closed the door in his face. He waited a week in half to contact me. I did not answer. This man I did something sexually with that I thought I would never do. He never asked me to, I desired to do it and enjoyed it. I remember one incident involving this same man. I was with my "pay master" (man), and he did not have the equipment to satisfy any normal women. He had the equipment of a little boy, need I say more. When I was with him, I had to fake it. He was good to me. He took me to places that I had never been to in my hometown. He spent money on me as well as giving me money. An incident comes to mind, after being with the "pay master," I quickly cleaned myself and invented an excuse to get rid of him. I told him I had to work the next morning. He bought it because he knew I worked two full-time jobs. Immediately when he left, I called the married man. Our well-known code for most lovers was 911 6969. He immediately called me back and said what was up. I asked him how soon you can get here. He said I am around the corner. I can be there in three minutes. He was at his mother-in law's house. I knew that because my mother went to a party at her house, and she found out that it was his mother-in-law's house. He came within the time he said. I cleaned myself a second before he came. I stayed naked. I did not put on anything. When he came, I stood behind the door and let him in. He was smiling and stating, "that is what I am talking about, Wow." Poor guy he did not even know that just ten to fifteen minutes ago I just had sex with my "pay master," and I was so frustrated that I had to have something I could feel. He arose quickly. It was on and popping. The "pay master" had a mad skill in oral sex. I admit I had never experienced an orgasm before him during oral sex. My mother wanted me to marry him. I told her no mama. I would be cheating on him, I could never be faithful Plus unlike you mom, I will never allow a man to come before my child, he does not like my son, so he do not like me. He called my son spoiled and he was not at that time. My son was not accustomed to having a man around me other than his father. It was just me and him before my mother moved. A couple of years later after the relationship had ended with "pay master." "Pay master" apologized to me and said that his son did him the same way my son had done him. When a child is not used to having a different sex around their parent, they get territorial. They are making sure they are number one in their parents' lives compared to a stranger just coming around.

I was a female, but I thought like a man. I also had control like a man. I made sure all the guys I was dating knew that I was single, and I saw who I wanted. Two of the three guys gave me the rules that they wanted me to abide by: if you see me out in public with me someone do not approach me or look as if you know me. I was excited because they dug a hole for themselves. I was not looking for a long-term relationship. I knew guys had a tendency of falling for me quickly, even if they were with someone else. This made mind manipulation easy for me. I told the two good, and I expect you to do the same whether you with your lady or not. From time to time, I would rehearse this in each one of their ears, even my baby daddy. I never fell in love with my baby daddy, which was not the norm in my days, I just wanted a baby boy.

An Incident comes to mind. I came home one afternoon, and my mother had found my spare black book of my male friends, and she had been calling each one and having them to bring over what she decided she wanted. She would tell each one what they wanted to hear, that I really liked them and wanted to be with them, but I worked too hard and did not have time to spend with them. My mom had called over the "pay master," and they were sitting in my living room when I arrived home. I spoke to both when I entered the apartment. I walked past them, went into my room and then to the bathroom to refresh myself and change clothes. I dressed and began to walk to the front door to leave and said, "you all have a good evening." My mother said, "Tonya, don't you see CC?" I looked directly at CC, pointed my finger, and said, "You did not call me, did you?" He said, "No I did not. I proceeded to walk out the door and go on my date with the married man. When I came back home. My mother was sitting in my lounge chair, drinking my liquor, and smoking a cigarette. I walked in and said, "Hey momma," before I could get to my room, my mother told me wait a minute. I stopped to see what she wanted. She said, "Tonya, you are a bad Bitch, I never did no shit like what you did today." We both laughed. I told my mother and just wait until tomorrow; the "pay master" will call tomorrow and ask to take me out and I will allow you to hear it. Sure enough, he called the next evening and asked me did I had an enjoyable time, and I said yes, I did. He then said, "So when can I take you out?" I asked him when you want to take me out. He told me and we went out. I allowed mother to listen to the conversation. She was amazed.

I used to be in committed relationships until my first adult boyfriend stalked me for almost two years. I never cheated on him. I just wanted out of the relationship. I would start off conversation with we are more of friends than anything and attempt to tell him I wanted to break it off. I was not seeing anyone else, but I was tired of the relationship. I had also had a spiritual visitation that told me he was not the one for me. The visit took place while I was on a long trip on a city bus to college. It was early in the morning, and I was the only one left on the back of the bus. In those two years after breaking up with him, he did the following: Once he put sugar in a gas tank. On two separate occasions: my ex-boyfriend cut my car tires, sprayed paint, and poured pink paint on my car twice. On another occasion, my ex-boyfriend broke into my room and took all my clothes; shoes and college books and snatched my phone of the hook; Tapped my phone lines and replayed all my calls by on my answering machine; car chased me; appeared in random places to invoke fear. The last incident was when he came to my apartment where I lived with my son's father with a female that he thought had been my friend to make me jealous. That did not work. I had moved on and the female and I were never friends. At the time my ex came to my apartment, my son was about two months old. My only concern was for the safety of my infant son.

The ex-boyfriend and this female that he thought was my friend had been lovers prior to our relationship but neither of us knew until our relationship was about to end and he asked how I met my son's father. I told him. My ex went on to inquire about who was the person I went to step show with. Told him her name and he then said, well did "T" tell you that me and her use to "Fuck." My response was no, she did not, but she did not know I was dating you in the beginning. I went on to say, "What you just said does not mean anything because she was not a friend to me, only someone I had only just met and was getting to know. The only thing stopped this mentally ill man from Terrorizing me was the last visit I had to the courthouse to speak to a district attorney. The injunction was not worth the paper it was on, until talked to the district attorney that had a separate case on my ex-boyfriend with another female. She told me to go home and that I never have to worry about him again. I never had a problem again.

First Spiritual Encounter

THROUGH ALL THAT I was doing, I was still talking to God. I used to ride city transportation to college, and it was a long journey weekly. I would drift off to sleep as soon as my mind was clear. I was not in a bible type relationship with God. I was still talking to him in my head on a regular basis to help me stand, finish my education so I could take care of myself, I had no one on whom I could depend. A still soft voice, said, "He's not the one for you." It scared me. I jumped up, looked around the back of the city bus and there was no one there but me. The voice was so real that it sounded like someone was on the back of the city bus speaking to me. The very next morning when going to college the same incident happens. This visitation reminds me of time this situation happened to Samuel the prophet of the bible, me too being young and not knowing the voice of God. The second time this happened when the spiritual manifestation happened, I was calm and just said yes, "Lord." Later that day, going to classes, I asked the Lord, how do I end the relationship (ex-boyfriend that began to stalk me after I finally ended relationship). God was with me to get out of that relationship.

Turbulence

THERE IS MORE to this life event as well. There was an incident that happened between my ex-boyfriend and baby daddy to be. My boyfriend doubled back after he left my house, and I had my son's father over. We have not had a child yet. Both guys got into a word, Boeing up at each other. I slipped around them, went out the front door of the rooming house, my cousin's father's house. Went down the street to Ms. Louise house, knocked on the door, asked for a pillow and her couch. She said what was wrong. I told her that my boyfriend that I had been trying to get rid of was at my house about to fight my new friend. She said what? I told her again. She gave me a pillow; I went to sleep right away. I woke up the next morning and went home. My family was a little worried about me but knew I was not too far. A second incident happened with the new boyfriend versus someone that was trying to become my boyfriend. My son's father had left me alone the first time because my ex-boyfriend confronted him about me. On this second incident my son's father and I spent the night together in my new apartment. The new boyfriend was married, and I did not know it. I knew something was not right about him. In general, I did not like married men and was not my choice to date them. I knew the new guy was hiding something. I asked him up front if he was married, and he said no. I was never vested in him because I knew he was hiding something. He gave me his friends, a couple's number to call him and I thought that was weird. I asked him why he gave them their number, and he said because he was temporarily living with them until his apartment came through, that he had just got out of a troubled relationship where he lived with someone. I laid the law down about the rules of our interactions. I told him that he sees who he wants, and I see who I want. The guy asked me if I was seeking someone else and I told him that that was none of his business and he was not to ask those types of questions. I kept asking him if he could handle the rules, and he said yes. I told him that we would get along if he abided by the rules. He tried to leave pieces of his clothing at my apartment, and I would make sure he took them with him. From time to time, I had to remind him that we are not in a committed relationship and that he could see who he wants, and I would do the same. He would ask, "are you seeing anyone? I would say that is none of your business. Do you want to end this now? He would say no. I would say so do not ask those questions. He tried leaving pieces of his garments at my apartment. I would tell him, "You are leaving your hat or whatever items, take it with you. He would say, "it can stay here until I get back," I said no sir. Take your belongings with you. Besides, I did not feel him like that. He went to jail; his old classmate called me and told me he and his wife had gotten into it. I told her, I knew he was hiding something, but it is ok because I was never into him. She apologized to me stating she thought I knew and that she encouraged him to tell me. I told her that she had nothing to apologize for because the relationship was not serious at all. While I was talking to her, I was in bed with my son's father, who resurfaced in my life once again.

The guy got out of jail for domestic violence with his wife and made a B line to my apartment. He knocked on my door and my son's father were still with me. My son's father stated here we go again. Tonya, what are you doing to these guys? I told him that it was ok and that he would go away because I made it clear we were just friends. My son's father said this dude is going to break in. I again restated that I made it clear we were just friends and nothing else. My son's father had enough time to get fully dressed and waited on the guy to break into my apartment. I was still in bed undressed. I slid the compartment to my bed headboard open and reached for my gun, took the safety off, and pointed it at my bedroom door. My son's father did not know I had a gun. The guy broke in and came to my bedroom door and saw my son's father and me pointing a gun at him. He threw me a watch he had bought me for Christmas that I was not expecting and did not ask for and walked back out of my apartment. My son's father said this is the second time I have gotten caught up and almost having to fight another guy. I apologized to him and said both times I was nothing to the relationships. The first time that happened I was trying to break up with my boyfriend and he kept avoiding me trying to end our relationship and the second time it was someone that was just a friend and I had made it clear that it was nothing more.

Confessing My Faith

WHEN I BECAME a Christian, I wanted to make sure it had stuck so to say. I had seen so many people over the years become Christians and then go back to living life and forgetting they had gone to the alter and gave there life over to God. I waited a while to tell my beloved aunt that I had gotten saved because I wanted her to be happy and rejoice with me. I remember when I got up the gumption to tell her. I told her aunt "X," I am saved now. Her response was you must have the Holy Ghost. I was devastated. I said to myself, "See I cannot do this, "I am not really saved, my beloved aunt "X" said that I am not saved," and she is the highest example of a saved person I have ever known. This Aunt believes in a Holy kiss. It took me years to be comfortable with my aunt kissing me on the cheek. When you come into her home, you must speak and give her a hug and allow her to kiss you on the cheek. I thought this was the most disgusting thing a person would ever experience beside her son molesting me and my mother trying to get me to sit with a 34-year-old man when I was only 14 years old. Besides my grandfather, this aunt gave me genuine love in her actions toward me. She did not know that her son had been molesting me until late in my early adulthood. In their family, incest was the norm. My two first cousins had a child with one another. The family eventually allowed it to come out later. In their family the men sometimes want to be females for years then, turn around and be males and have children. And the cycle repeats itself.

Tragedy

MY BELOVED BROTHER "Mickey Mouse" died in a fatal car accident, and my youngest brother was in the accident with him. The youngest brother stayed in a coma for about two weeks. He was not able to attend his brother's funeral. No one told him that Mickey Mouse was deceased. We all tried to keep it from him as long as we could. "Mickey Mouse," birth name "Hubert Jim lord Jackson" was my maternal mother's middle child. I gave him the nickname, Mickey Mouse. He was a pretty baby but very nosy. His ears would perk up when people would talk around him. He would turn his ear in the direction that adults were talking, so he could hear conversations. Mickey Mouse could not even crawl, walk or stand but he would listen. Mickey Mouse's father was from Jamaica. His father married my mother. My stepfather father loved to be with more than one woman. My stepfather was an incredibly provider and the best father I ever had. He was highly intelligent, wise, and patient when it came to business and children. My mother married my stepfather so that he could stay in the United States. My mother had been marring men like this to get paid by them so they can stay in the states. One of my cousins on my biological father's side of the family taught my mother the ropes and got paid. My stepfather sold marijuana. Back then a nickel bag was inch up from the bottom of a plastic lunch bag and going straight across the bag. My stepfather was exported back to Jamaica for selling marijuana. About 20 years or so later, my stepfather was killed at gun point walking out of another's man's house. He had been sneaking around with the man's women. When my stepfather came out to fight; the man shot him in the head.

Robbed

DURING MY MOTHER'S marriage to my stepfather, she was robbed at gunpoint with me and my brother in the house. Me and my brother had not lived with our mother for a brief time when this happened. My brother and I was not used to this kind of lifestyle even though no transactions were done at home, but we knew where the marijuana was hidden: a big Red Giant Vase with a Black dragon on it. My mother was seven or eight months pregnant with our little sister. Two men came in with women stocking caps over their faces with guns in their hands. My mother begged then men to allow us to go into our rooms. They eventually did. As a little girl around five or six, I prayed for my mother's safety. The guys got what they came for weed and whatever money was in the house. My mother called out to us saying we can come out now. When I came out of the room, my mother was walking outside of the house to sit in a chair. It was summer. When my mother began to sit down, my God mother she picked for me came around the corner talking loudly, saying "Hazel, I heard what happen." My mother got up out her chair on the front porch and began walking toward my God mother saying, "you heard?" See, it was impossible for my God mother to have heard that my mother was robbed because the men had just run out of our apartment just seconds before she arrived. I mean seconds!

My mother then paused in her conversation with my God mother and began to walk slowing towards her. My mother got close to my God mother, grabbed her by her hair and began to punch and beat her down. She held on to her with one hand by her hair while she punched her in her face and stomach a couple of times. My mother told my God mother she could not have heard that quick because it had just happened within seconds. My mom had just sat down outside within minutes of the men who robbed her left, when God mother came around corner stating Hazel, I heard what happened. My mother had stayed her distance from my God mother sense the dope needle incident.

Dope Needle Incident!

GOD MOTHER AND my mother as mentioned above had a situation about a dope needle. A few years earlier, they rode to a bar to buy dope to shoot in their veins. I was still living with my grandparents and normally was not allowed to go anywhere with my biological mother. On this day I was allowed to go with her. She wanted to take me off and I was not so comfortable with that, but I went along. My mother gave my God mother the money to go inside the bar to buy the dope and come back and they share using it. It was an extremely hot summer. Me and my mother sat in the car sweating with the windows down. We waited a while. As a young child not even in grade school, I began to think about how long my God mother had been in the bar. I talked to God and said she has been in there too long and have used all the dope that she had bought. What is she going to tell my mother when she comes out? If she comes out. My God mother eventually came out and sat in the car. She pulled out the needle that was supposed to be dope: heroin. I intuitively knew that the syringe had water in it. I prayed to God not to allow my mother to shoot up the water in her veins to protect her. When my mother began to shoot the water into her veins she instantly stopped and grabbed for my God mother stating, "Bitch this is water!" She ran from my mother and my mother stopped talking to her for a while and never trusted her again.

Prior to this incident, this woman and her child stayed with my grandparents, my mother and us for a year until she was able to get on her feet and she goes and set my mother up to be robbed during her pregnancy. My mother was a street-smart woman. She knew she could not trust my God mother so I would think she would not have known where the weed was unless She, herself had slept with my stepfather, got him drunk and he accidentally told her where he keeps his stash. This was the kind of women this was. My God mother was a very gorgeous, charming, and shapely women. Her skin was beautiful. You can only tell her age by her hair. It had thin out over the years of dying it blonde. They say that she was not always a loose woman. She came from up north, a very smart young girl with her sister and their father. They said she got turned out while in high school by a guy that was no good. They say that she was wild ever sense then. This woman began to school her daughter about men around 11 or 12 years old. My mother was still young, but she told her that she was wrong to start teaching her daughter so young how to use men and things about sex. I overheard their conversation. I found that ironic because, when I lived with my grandparents, mother mother/big sister told me so much about having a cycle and sex that it almost blew my child mind. I was only about five or six years old. I had to pray to my imaginary friend, "God" to hold my mind together. I was not ready for what she shared with me. In my mother's defense, she told me because her own mother never told her anything. She did not know about having a cycle, sex, or too much of anything that would have kept her safe and or prepared. At Four to five years old I learned about makeup. I would sit by my big sister/ mother and watch her put on her make up. She was highly skilled in putting on makeup like the models. She also put on eyelashes.

Getting over My First Adult Boyfriend/Stalker

I HAD A warning in my spirit not to date him. Months later "dude" called me, and I forgot about the first bad gut feeling of not dating him. I began to date him over the phone, too scared to date in person because I did not want to get pregnant. I am the oldest of seven. After dating a guy for a while. We planned to have sex. He took me over to his sister's house because she and her old man was going out to the club. The two siblings purposely left me and sister's old man alone in living while they were in bedroom talking with door closed. We both sat in the living room for what seemed forever in a day trying to avoid talking, much less looking at each other so as not to give the wrong impression. Eventually, after thirty minutes to an hour we began to talk respectfully. Neither one of us was interested in one another. There were no books or TV to watch to keep us pre-occupied. We had a decent respectful conversation but kept them short. We both ended up laughing, still not interested in one another. The siblings: my new boyfriend and his sister came out of the room both cursing at each one of us. I looked very startled, confused, and decided that I was ready to go back home. The sister walked out of her apartment with her boyfriend, and I began to walk behind them. My new boyfriend stopped me and told me that I was not going "no damn where." I sat down. I thought to myself, I do not understand this, he does not know me to have accused me of talking to the guy as if I was interested? I then thought this guy is crazy and I need to think of a way of getting out of this situation. I looked around and burglar bars were all around the apartment, including the doors. He had locked me in. I learned a lot living with my mother, especially when she was in an abusive relationship with one of my stepfathers. I knew how to watch my surroundings and always had a planned escape route. He steadily cursed and hit me on my head with his hand and fingers. I did what became natural after watching my mother all those years in one of her marriages where my stepfather beat her all the time. I began to talk calmly and smile and tried to touch him to soothe his anger. I could not tell if it worked or not. Told him I wanted to go home. He told me he is not taking me home. I sat in the living room for about an hour. He went into the bedroom. I prayed so hard, "God do not let me die. Please let me make it to see another day. Lord, no one knows where I am. This guy could kill me and dispose my body, and no one knows him or where I went. My nerves were on edge. He came out of the room and demanded that I come into the room. I said I was ok where I was. He demanded me to come into the room. I walked into the room and sat on the bed, shaking like a leaf, wanting to go home. I knew not to ask him to take me home anymore because he functioned as if he was going to start hitting me again. He then told me to take off my clothes. I did as he asked, shaking like a leaf. Once my clothes were off, he pushed me back into the bed and got on top of me. Mind you, I had never had a sexual experience with a man before other than my older cousin fondling me with his fingers and objects. I said to myself, he can do whatever he wants as long as I live. It was painful on top to him and me, but I was taking it. He decided to flip me on my back, and it was less painful. I went to the bathroom afterwards to clean up. Still scared. He told me to lie down. I did not sleep all night. I wanted to live. That morning, he took me home. All night I said if

I live to see another day, I will kiss the grown and tell God thank you, I will never go anywhere else without someone knowing where I am, how long I am to be gone and with whom I went with. No one ever warned about situations like this. I always wanted a big sister. One may have come in handy prior to this date rape situation.

Getting over Relationship with Son's Father

I WAS NEVER in love with this guy, just wanted a baby boy child. I would have someone again that loved me unconditionally like my grandfather did. This guy had a drug problem. He smoked marijuana and snorted cocaine powder. He had been through two situations where my ex and friendship broke in on us while we were together. We met at an EWC step show. He was a handsome, tall, bright skinned guy. I was not interested in him at all. I was out with a female that knew me from college. I did not know her very well and did not feel comfortable with her. It was something about her that unsettled me in my spirit. I knew to be on guard with her. My son's father kept trying to talk to me. I eventually gave him a small conversation, did not want to be mean. I did not want to be with him, but I was taught not to be mean, you never know when you will need someone. We exchanged phone numbers. We got through those missed haps with the two other guys. We end up living together. We both had decent jobs. I was still in college towards the end of earning my four-year Degree in Sociology, Social Welfare. My favorite Aunt "X" had told me at my cousin's wedding reception once that my son's father would make no women a good husband until he give his heart fully over to Christ. I was too ashamed to tell my aunt that I never intended on marry this man in the first place. I knew he was not my husband or the type of man I wanted to marry in the first place, I just wanted a baby boy and once I got what I wanted, I needed to find a way of getting rid of him. As far as paying bills, I decided I would take care of the rent because I wanted control to if he acted out, I would put him out. He was responsible for the lights and phone bills and other necessities. Him, having a drug habit, I found myself allowing him to borrow money. He promises to pay me back. He pays me back never happened. One time his ex-girlfriend had his car taken. He was not paying for the car note. I was still in college, and it was time for my student loans to come out. He knew this. He begged me and talked to me constantly to allow him to borrow money to get his car out of pound. He told me about one figure and then produced another figure. To get his car out of the pound took up the whole amount of my student loan. I got a book check separate from that, so I did not have to worry about my college books. I was going to use the funds to purchase furniture that I needed badly. He promised to pay me back and never did.

Baby

FOR YEARS, I never wanted children because I was the oldest of seven siblings. When I turn twenty-four, I began to desire a male child. He would grow up to be a significant help and or protector to his mother. Previously, in the past, my first fiancé, I cut off an engagement with a military guy that always talked about having children like his brother because I did not want kids right away. I stopped taking my birth control pills and after while I got pregnant and my son's father told me I was pregnant, that I needed to "get checked out" by my doctor and I was. I was still in college in what was supposed to be my last semester. I would get morning sickness an hour before the end of my math class. I counted that as a blessing then. I could hang in there for an hour. My math class was late in the evening, so the sickness came around 5pm. I was concerned about my baby because I had just found out through his father's maternal sister that his father had a history of cocaine abuse. She kept hinting around at first asking me where her brother's money is going, she would ask: "have you ever wondered what he does with his money, why did you have to use so much of your student loan to get his car out of pound, what was he doing with his money." I tried marijuana one time after being persuaded by a friend to smoke with her in middle school and did not like it. I never smoked anything again nor use any type of drugs by the grace of God. Drug abuse and alcohol abuse were in my blood line, and I saw at too young of age what it does to people. I made a vow that I would never use drugs or drink alcohol to cope. I did not want anything or no one to have control of me. When I had my son, he was exceedingly small, 5lbs and 7 ounces. The doctor and nurses kept asking if I used drugs or smoked. I was incredibly angry about them questioning me like this. It came to me that I always looked noticeably young for my age and that something may have come up because my son father used drugs. He smoked marijuana every day. I did not know how often he used cocaine. He always got good jobs to support his habits and to have him a nice car to ride in.

The Breakup

I BROKE UP with my son's father because he jumped on me. He was going through withdrawals because he and been to every "drug hole" for weed and no one had any. My son was crawling then and to my knowledge did not talk. He had no reason too because I was a good mother. I had him on my schedule. He was always clean, dressed as a nice happy baby. My son did not cry unless he hurt himself badly. My son's father got mad at me because I was trying to hurry up and prepare the baby something to eat when we got back home. Quinton said "eat, eat momma, eat- eat." I had never heard my son say any words before other than his first words, "Dadda." I rushed and tried to fix him something to eat. His father came into the kitchen and said he can eat when we eat. I tried to explain to my son's father that his grandmother's microwave was old and by the time the rock-hard chicken thawed out, I would have cooked our son three meals. I made this statement calmly to him to get him to understand. He yelled at me and said, "I said he can wait and eat with us. Oh boy! Something reared up in me. It could have been when my mother was with the stepfather that was very abusive to her. She would feed him first the best food and drink, while us kids got lima beans, rice, and water. I told my son's father, let me tell you something, my son is hungry, you kept us out running the streets for that junk, my child comes first, and I am going to feed my son. He came after me to beat me. I took a black cast iron frying skillet, swung at him, and missed. We began to fight toe to toe at first. My son was crawling around our legs crying. This incident ended the relationship. I had told all my boyfriends if they ever put their "hands on" me that would be the end of it. My son's father started pushing me at first when we would have disagreements. He would always say, I did not hit you afterwards. My sons self-made God mother called my house while I was locked in bathroom to avoid my son's father fighting me. I answered the phone but would not say anything. She got the message. I have never seen anyone get to my house so quickly that they stayed so far away in my life. My son and I left with her that night. The next morning her boyfriend invited my son's father over to their apartment. None of the guys cared for my baby father but suddenly, her boyfriend invited him over. Part of the problem was that my son's father never liked sharing his weed, but he would lie and say he did not have anything to bring over to the house party. My son's self-made called God mother told me that her boyfriend had invited my son's father over her apartment. I got up and began to get my items together to leave. She said you do not have to go anywhere, and I said I did. So, I went back to my duplex to pack his clothes and to take them over to his mother's home. She and another childhood girlfriend rode with me. I was Quiet, but they were talkative. They made comments stating that we would be back together again. I got tired of hearing it and read them their rights: You are the one that let your man come on your job and beat you down in front of your co-workers and you allow your man to cheat on you with other women and you know all the details, but you keep taking him back. I tell both of you today, our family has a pattern, once we are done with a relationship and when we say we are done, the relationship is over. They were both quite for a minute but changed the topic. When we got to his mother's apartment. No one was home. I looked at her car. My childhood friend said, "check and see if her car door open, that is his mother's car, right?' I said yes. Checked the doors and the back door was open. I piled all his clothes into his mother's car and locked it. I then called him and told him that he would not come back to my house where I pay rent. He said that it is my house too, I pay bills there too and I am coming home. Told him that my cousins would be waiting for him, and he said I have cousins too. I said OK, all I am saying, I do not want you back there at all. The very next week I paid $25.00 to put my son's father on child support. I never went back to him. I used him for money from time to time. I got more money out of him during that time than us being in a so-called committed relationship. He was never committed. I caught him in two different situations. I did not trust his mother because I thought she was phony. She loved me because I was an educated women going somewhere in life, and she wanted me with her son. Over the years I have grown to have respect and love for her despite her ways.

Ending a Relationship

PRIOR TO GETTING married. I was a woman who maintained three men, worked two full time jobs and was a leader on both jobs. I was my daytime manager's boss on our second job. We both had mutual respect and neither of us crossed the line. I fail in love with one of the men I was seeing. It was the married man that I found out was getting a divorce. One of my co-workers had seen in at the courthouse with his paperwork to get a divorce. He never mentions it to me. He was one of three guys I saw that was interested in what I read and wanted to know how I thought so he would read and discuss the books I read. Game, right? I invited him over the Dynasty as he called it to enjoy one another and to talk. Before things got moving. I talked with him while he was sitting on a higher step on my staircase and I was on the lowest, laying on my back, teasing him because I did not have on any under clothes. I came right out like a man would and said I had feelings for him, and he said he liked me too. I went on to say that I was falling in love with him. I had the nerve to do so because I heard he was getting a divorce from his wife. His response was quiet. I asked him did he hear what I said. He said he did, and I said so? He said he cares about me. I told him to come on and tell me the truth, I can handle it. So, he told me he did not feel the same way about me. Wow, a truly tall, built, nice looking, professional, dark as midnight Black man turn me down. No, I did not get a complex against dark Black men. They just never were into me as I was into them. The light skinned, funny eyed, Black men chased me down like a bear hunting honey. So, after he told me that he does not feel the same as me. I jumped onto another subject of conversation with him. Counted down in my head. My next move was to take him up- stairs and have sex with him and afterwards create a reason for him to leave when I was finish with him. When I finished with him, I told him I had to go to work early on my second job the next day and I must call it a night. I made the statement as soon as I finished having sex with him. I went to the bathroom to get myself together and walked him downstairs to the front door. He walked out the front door. I stood there with doorknob in my hand and began to tell him, with door almost closed, "by the way, we are done, don't call me anymore or beep me." He said, "What? Just like that?" and I said yes and closed the door, went upstairs, and took a bath and went to sleep without any remorse or thinking about what I had just done. I did not lose any sleep over it at all. He called me a week later and I did not answer the phone nor beep. I had let the other two guys go a couple of weeks earlier. I started feeling like I wanted my own man, a husband, a family. I was thinking of this man some- one I could see myself with. I knew how to please him, and I knew what position to take to please myself with him. Side bar: I dis- covered later in life, in my mid-forties that quite a few women have not experienced their "G" spot organism. I was amazed at that. I had a close relative in her late forties that had just experienced hers and wanted to share. I told her wow; I have experienced what you just have years ago, beginning in my early thirties. I had an older women friend in her fifties that had never experience an organism it. She married her high school sweet- heart and had children from same man? I tried to educate her about positions, but her ears were not open all the way to comprehend what I was trying to teach her. She saw me as a baby and she herself as older, wiser, and conservative.

First Marriage Experience

WHEN I GOT pregnant, he was so happy. I was a small woman to him, and he liked full figured women. He tried to feed me potatoes and all kinds of stuff to fatten me up. Now a baby. He wanted a little boy, and he wanted to see more weight on me. At the time I was between size twelve and fourteen. Obesity runs in my mother's family, I did not want to get big and experience heart problems, high blood pressure. I did not want to be big ever. We dealt with the fact he did not want to move to Jacksonville even though he adamantly stated he would move prior to us getting married. He came to Jacksonville to visit from time to time. I did not know he was under investigation for illegal activities. I had heard the rumor. He was arrested and charged. He kept telling me that he would be out soon, and he was sentenced to time in prison. My world came tumbling down. I was hurting at the fact that I did not want to raise another male child without his father's help. I had a young son that I planned, and I felt the mistake of my error in just wanting a baby and not the father of the baby. The thought tore me up and I began to think I do not want this child. "As a man thinketh so is he." I began to sink into a deep depression about having another child without help physically and financially. My mind was in total turmoil. I began to have suicidal tendencies again. I had a gun and would often time play with it but could never put the gun to my head to pull the trigger. I read and studied the Bible from the beginning to the end for answers. I asked the "Lord why was this happening to me?" When I got married, I wanted it to be forever. I told God, I want out of this. He is not what he said he was. After I married him, things changed. He lied to get me as a trophy. As time progressed, I cried all the time. I sink deeper and deeper into depression. I had a roommate. The one was responsible for getting into church and searching and developing a relationship with God. I walked off my job, The Department of Children and Families as a foster Care counselor. I have been with the department for seven years. I started this career after I graduated from college. I applied for public assistance. My mortgage at the time was only $434.00 a month. With Aid to Family with Children, AKA AFDC, and the funds my roommate gave me I paid the mortgage and light bill. I would go without eating or drinking for prolonged periods of time. I would close my bedroom door and would not come out for a day or two. My roommate would take care of my son and check on me. At times I would lay on the cold shower floor with my big belly and wish to die. I had concluded that I could not take my life because that was an unforgiveable sin, and my eternal life would be lived out in Hell. I would go to church with my roommate and when I entered the door I would cry deeply. The Pastor asked me what was wrong. I could not tell him, but it upset him so much. At one point he said he knew that the baby inside of me was dead through God showing it to him, but he could not bring himself to telling me that because of the grief and the state of mind I was in. My husband is in prison, with no income and no family support. My town home's air conditioner had gone out. I am big and pregnant. My roommate and I would go to the mall to get air because it would get so hot in the house.

When I went to Shand's hospital, I had to wait for approval from Medicaid to see a doctor. My roommate asked me when the last time the baby moved. I told her I did not know. She called to see if I could get an earlier appointment and Shand's Hospital said no, they were booked up. So, when it finally came to seeing the doctor. He told me that my baby was dead and that I would have to give birth to the baby the next day because of my insurance. They told me to go home and prepare myself for the next day. So, I went home as instructed and told my roommate. I went into my bedroom and began to cry all over again, now for the loss of my baby. The next day, I went alone. My roommate said she just could not go; she had borne so much of my grief she just could not bear this. So, I went alone. I called my babysitter and told her about it. She was my babysitter for my son from three months old until grade school. She asked me if there was anyone with me and I said no. She said she would send this person that had never spoken to me, and she kept her son as well for years. I did not like this person because she has a, "I am better than all other parents' attitude," so she did not speak to anyone when she came to pick her son up but the babysitter. Over the years, I would tell my babysitter that if this person ever looked at me or did anything to offend me, I was going to beat her Ass. Getting back on topic, I told my babysitter that I did not need anyone with me to deliver my stillborn son. My babysitter sent this woman anyway. My babysitter uses to tell me, "Tonya stop being so mean, you never know who you might need to bring you a glass of water."

This woman showed up and was compassionate toward me for the first time in years of seeing over to the babysitter's house picking up our boys. I was finally visible to her on account of our babysitter. This woman held my hand as I gave birth to my deceased son. My son was pale greyish in color. He had a head covered with black hair. This is just one of two Life-or-death situations I have encounter. I do not know how long this baby has been dead inside of me. I could have died from this. After being released from the hospital, the women, the babysitter sent came out to my house to check on me. And guess what? She had to bring me a glass of water from my kitchen. When she visited my house, her disposition was beginning to change toward me. At first, she was surprised that I had a home with the type of items I had in it. I was very upscale when it came to furniture and décor in my home. I can only imagine what she was thinking, "I thought she was "ghetto?" I never would have thought she lived in this neighborhood and her home looked like this. I lived in a neighborhood with Caucasians and one other black professional. I have always talked to people of all levels of society and been compassionate. And just as I have mentioned earlier, Black people get to the point where they carry themselves as if others are beneath them and I had a problem with that for years. Now, I pay it no mind, but I do not allow a lower-class person to be embarrassed or degraded while I am around. I will go and serve that person as much as is wise and able to do. I know where I come from, and I have a compassionate heart.

Testimony of My Walk with God

I AND MY younger cousin are ten years apart in age and her mother is ten years older than I. My youngest cousin is just like her mother in ways but not all. God blessed my cousin that I am 10 years older, to watch me through the struggle I was going through. She never put me down or talked hard to me. She had a friend that knew the bible like the back of her hand but was not living it. I was in the process of learning the bible, but my demeanor and attitude was different than my cousin's bible knowledgeable friend. My cousin told me she compared her friend to me and saw a big difference. My walk with God, made her curious about God. She was mad at God for taking her father early and sometimes, she did not believe in God. She asked me questions about my relationship with God. I answered her questions the best I could. By her watching my new change, it sparked her interest to learn more about this God, Jesus Christ person and the Holy Ghost. She began to read on her own and had questions ready for me that sometimes I could answer and sometimes I could not. The result she gave her life over to Jesus Christ and received a heavy anointing in the Prophetic gifting. She could read things about people like a book. Her gift was so strong. It exceeded mine and I was good with that and thanked God for blessing and using her so. After watching me go through the darkest areas of my life, my young cousin told me that I needed to find someone I halfway trust to talk to because I hold too much on the inside and it will come a day if I do not let some of this out, it would destroy me. I took her advice. I choose my babysitter, an older woman. All the other young women talked to her, but she kept their business and did not tell other parents.

    I went to visit my cousin twice a week, not for her gift but I loved her daughter. Her daughter and I had a special bond, and she brought peace to me when I was not feeling so good emotionally. Her daughter was and is slightly disabled. On one visit I remembered my cousin asking me to come into her room and she needed to talk to me. I had been praying asking God, why all these things keep happening to me. My life is miserable. I always have had to scratch and claw for things I needed and wanted. Why do things always come hard to me? She told me something that I did not remember, and it made me see her in a different light: this is truly an Old Testament prophet of God. It was something I told God when I was a little girl. She even told me where I was standing and what was in front of me when I told God that I would take on the calamities of people's suffering. She told me I was in my grandparents' living room watching TV. I was floored, how God could reveal such a thing to her and an event I had forgotten about. She went on to tell me that is why you go through so much Hell because you asked for it. Right at that moment, I was about to get mad until the spirit calmed me down and let me know not to get mad at the Holy Spirit because it is truth that is spoken. I never thought of getting mad at my cousin, but the Holy Ghost and I were about to be on dangerous grounds.

I told my cousin, venting, He cannot hold me accountable for that, I did not know what I was asking and praying for at that time, I was only a small child. She said very sweetly and lowly, but he heard you and honored your request. My mind was totally blown. All this time and what I been through and yet must walk through, is because of what I said as a child watching the Ethiopian children starving and other situations on TV. I was a happy, loved, and secure child living with my grandparents and I felt so much compassion for others' situation in Africa and on the news, really? It took time to get use to this but eventually I accepted it as I grew in the knowledge of God. How can you help deliver someone to get free from certain things and you yourself have not experienced too much adversity in life. Or have not gone through anything. The events mentioned so far are only the tip of the ice berge.

Evil Stepfather

I HAVE ALWAYS been a loner although I was always well known in the public eye. My outward appearance, good looks, innocent calm demeanor with my Godly glow attracted people from a small age all the way into adulthood. Even with these qualities, I had anger issues, unforgiveness inside of me. The anger and unforgiveness developed after I was remove from my grandparent's home after my grandmother died. The last man that I am aware my mother married was an abuser, the brother of at that time of my beloved aunt. I hated this man with a passion. He was on drugs unbelievably bad. He had spent a substantial amount of his life in prison. He was the youngest and the only male child of sisters. He would not work anywhere to save his life. He would not work on a pie train going to Georgia. He would have my mother work on a job while he would steal the nectar out of honey. His habit was Heroin. He would use needles to shoot this drug in his veins. He would go into a violent rage sometimes and accuse my mother of dating other men and or sleeping with other men. My mother was an incredibly beautiful woman, and he was a very unattractive man. He kept himself exceptionally clean, groomed, and neat. He always dressed genuinely nice but still he was a very unattractive man. He came from a family that believed in beating children like slaves. Me and my oldest siblings: Rodney and Mickey Mouse were from my mother's other relationships, and we did not know anything about being beat with extension cords and other hard-core items he would beat us with. We did not know anything about eating Lima beans, rice and having a glass of water Seven days a week, while all the best food was saved for our step farther. Our mother would cook and serve steak, nice veggies, sodas, or any other flavored drink my stepfather wanted. Me and my two brothers were accustomed to eating what kids like to eat and drinking whatever the adult was drinking. We never even know too much about Lima beans. Our grandparents ate them, but they never gave them to us to eat. My grandmother would cook several meal options, place them on table, and ask us which items we wanted, and we had to get a veggie along with other items and it had to be a balance in her eyesight. I do have to add that my mother had three children from this psychotic man. When I call him this, it does not mean I am still anger or have un-forgiveness toward this man, I am calling it what it was at that time because of his behavior while shooting up drugs.

The time my mother was with this man was a very dark time in my life and my older sibling's life. He would beat our mother until sometimes she would fall unconscious. My nerves were always on edge. In my mind, I had to always be alert, I always noted an escape route to go in case my stepfather went crazy, beating my mother, throwing furniture items, and more. One never knew when he was going to explode. The worst times were at night. I was a light sleeper from that time until my late thirties. I would wake up if I heard a cat walking outside meowing or just his footsteps hitting dried leaves on the grown. I remember one time this man went into an explosive rampage, and we all had to strike out running from him one night. My mother had left us older children that were not his by blood and we did not know, we only heard the noise and sat patiently trying to figure out if this was a mild fight or an out-of-control situation. Then he came into our room and started yelling. I and my two brothers made it to the front door. He caught up with us. I was behind my two brothers; I wanted them to get out first. I was the oldest child, and I always protected my siblings. He blocked the way, cursing, calling our mother all kinds of names and trying to convince us that our mother was just what he called her. All three of us just stood there looking, saying nothing, scared and shaking. He eventually knocked Rodney on the head with a wooden broom; we all took off and ran toward our grandfather's house. We made it to his house. We knew if we made it to his house, he would protect us. My grandfather loved guns. He had a raffle behind his bedroom door and front door. He had various other guns hidden in each part of his small, tiny home. All three of us ran the entire way to our grandfather's house without stopping. It was a mile to our grandfather's house from our house. Fear would give you the added strength to go the distance, especially when you have a lunatic, pumped up on heroin chasing you. When we got there, grandfather opened the door for us and calmed us down. He asked where our mother and the babies were. We told him we did not know that they were gone before we known anything. Grandfather told us that we had nothing to worry about, that we were with him now and that he would blow his brains out if he tried to hurt us. He went on to see if we were hungry or wanted something to drink and prepared what we asked him. When he finished looking after us, he sat by the front door with his pistol beside him. Our mother finally showed up with our twin siblings in a Winn-Dixie grocery buggy that our stepfather had taken home for me to use to take everyone in the household laundry to the laundry mat. Grandfather helped momma get the babies inside the house fussing all the way. He told my mother, why are you still with that no-good man. He is not a man; he does not work anywhere and do not help you do nothing. Grandfather was cursing hard. I cannot remember all the curse words he said.

I hated this abusive stepfather for years into my adulthood because of the abuse my mother suffered by him and the hardships he caused us to live in by not working and stealing all the time. He even made me crawl through a window to open another person's door to their home. I was only about eleven years old and did not want to do it but had no other choice. The family was out of town and someone in the neighborhood let him know, knowing what he was about, and they were too scared to break into the person's home. They made a deal, and it happened.

I prayed for days to God, my imaginary friend, not to allow me to be forced to climb through someone's home window so my stepfather could rob their home. God honored my request. He did not allow my stepfather to be put in a situation of breaking into someone's home or stealing. I can recall an incident of my stepfather's violent rage that happened in Valdosta Georgia. My stepfather tended to move us around to different cities. One night while the house was pitched dark and all of us were sleeping in the wee hours of the morning, suddenly, my stepfather began to punch and beat my mother in the bed next to us. She had slept with my other small baby's siblings' bed because he had gone out and she did not know when he was coming back. She told him she was going to sleep in the bed with the twin girls to wake her up when he gets in. He said OK. My mother screamed and told me to cut on the lights. My mother thought someone had broken in on us and was beating her. I jumped up and was afraid to cut on the lights. I did not know if this person that had broken in had a gun or what. I heard the punches my mother was taking.

Then I thought it was my stepfather that had gotten high again and was punching her. I did not know what to do. I got up because this man had dragged her into the living room beating her. I got to the living room, my mother cried out again, Tonya cut on the lights. By the second time she asked me to cut on the lights, my eyes had adjusted to the darkness so that I could see the silhouette of a man butt naked. I could not cut on the lights then because my stepfather was butt naked beating my mother badly. My stomach was in knots and pain. There was nothing I could do. I cried and prayed to God, please do not let him kill my mother this time. He could kill her this time. God please helps. My stepfather stopped for a moment and ran back into the bathroom which was to the back of the house and put on cut off shorts. He came back through the house cutting on lights. He asked me what happened to my mother, why was she lying in the middle of the dirt road. I did not say anything. What could I say? He then told me to go out and check on her. I could not bring myself to go out to check on her because I did not know if she was dead or alive. She was not moving. I went to call the ambulance. After this beating, my mother could not see out of her eyes for two weeks. Her eyes were swollen shut. My stepfather had punched her repeatedly in her eyes and face that she looked like the elephant man. I had to guide my mother around the house for two weeks until the swell of both of her eyes went down. I had to cook by her verbal directions for the whole house. When I came into my middle thirties, I got a revelation although I had not come into a covenant relationship with God, the father, Jesus, and the Holy Spirit yet. It was as if God dropped something in my spirit man and mind. I could not blame my abusive stepfather for beating my mother and causing us to live a lifestyle of lack because he did not want to work, but my mother was partly to blame. She had a choice to leave this abusive relationship. He went on to say that she was trapped in her mindset: six children, who would help her with all these children. Then it was the issue that her own brother by her mother but from another man, had raped her in the sugar cane fields of Clewiston Florida. My mother had even alluded to her father; my beloved grandfather had done something to her. She would never go into details about what grandfather did to her. After this revelation, I totally forgave my stepfather and began to ponder what could have happen in his childhood or prison for him to be the way he was besides not being a decent looking man. At that time, I had been out of college for a couple of years. I received a four-year degree in Sociology and minored in social welfare. I took pre-requisite courses in Psychology, how and why people do the things they do. One could say I was using the skills set that college had taught me to try to evaluate my stepfather.

After God dealt with me on this and brought deliverance in my sinful state: working two jobs and dating three men at one time. My stepfather called me while I was at work and began to talk to me. He tried to convince me to see things his way in a comment he made about my mother. I told him that was what you used to say when we all were together, and I never believed a word of that. Do you know what I thought when you said that? The cow really jumped over the moon too. There was no anger in my voice nor my emotions anymore. I told him that I do not hate him or hold anger against him because it took two, that my mother had a choice to leave you, but she did not. She stayed as long as she could because she loved you. We then both jumped onto another subject immediately. Eventually, my mother did leave only after a near death experience. During his last violent episode with her, he hit her on the back of her head with an old iron shovel. Yes, an Iron heavy wide shape shovel. She went into the hospital and the doctor saved her life and informed her that she had almost lost her life because a half inch more she would have been dead. The shovel left a large scare in her head.

College Experience

I HAD THIS Black professor at the University of North Florida that did not like me and would indirectly call me names to insinuate that I had mental problems. It got so bad that my classmates would know that he was talking about me. I still had anger issues at that time, but I chose my battles, and I allowed certain people not to move me to anger. I loved and enjoyed this professor's classes and the books he would have us read. I would take my time and write very neatly when he wanted a written response during class time, and I would know the materials that he had us to read like the back of my hand. Although, I did a fantastic job in all areas of requirements in his class. I was never late on an assignment; He would give me the lowest grade that he could without looking too ridiculous. I would take it. Most of my main courses I had to take with him. One time, I waited patiently to talk to him. I asked him, Mr. W, why do you always give me low ball grades when I know that I did better. His remark was, "I gave you what you earned." I said no sir, you did not but ok. I never approached him again until graduation day. His daughter and I were good friends, and he never knew. She marched even though she was not officially graduating because she had not finished a paper in a class from another professor even after extensions. She told me this as we marched in together. At the end of the ceremony, she demanded that I meet her father. I informed her that I was already acquainted with her father, as I had taken most of my courses under his instruction. She said I know but I want him to know who you are to me. I said OK. When his daughter introduced me to him as her good friend and her college mother, it was like someone had died, the look on his face. She said daddy, this is the friend I told you about. He was stunned. He knew he had treated me so badly for the two years I was at the University of North Florida. I did regret not informing a higher authority later in life when I wanted to go back to school but because of the grades this man gave me my GPA was the low. One could say God was developing me during me not being totally committed to Him. Molding and shaping me. And quite a few people think, especially Christian or Believers that God do not speak to or deal with sinner men. He spoke to a donkey to try to delay the prophet Bel from going to curse the children of Israel, so why cannot he speak and developed a sinner man. One of the things I find funny, is an old saying, "Get right while the blood still running warm in your veins." Sometimes because of all the serious stuff that has happened in a person's life, God must deal with him in the state that he is already in (the unknowing molding and shaping, prior to becoming one of his own).

Looking for Love in All the Wrong Places

I NEVER FELT loved being the eldest of seven children. My mother did not focus on me because she had so much to deal with as I have written thus far. I did not let my mother's life of attention trouble me as much as the molestation by my beloved aunt by marriage did or me thinking I was dumb because my mother called me dummy often. My mother got so tired of my teachers writing about my grades and my behavior. They would say she is not interested, or she needs testing for special education. These poor teachers did not know this little cute quite little girl had the weight of the world on her shoulders. My thoughts were preoccupied with, wonder if we will get put out tonight, will mom and stepdad have money to pay light bill, will stepdad kill my mother while I am in school today. Sometimes, I would have talked my mother into leaving my stepfather come back home and she had decided to stay with him. He was very manipulating and calculating. At any rate, I had low self-esteem. After being bombarded with teacher's notes and requests for a conference, mom started calling me dummy. That pushed me further down. I ended up in special Ed classes. After a year of being in this class, Mrs. Latimoore pushed me to be transferred out of her class because she said I did not belong there. Mrs. Latimoore observed me, finishing my work early while other kids were working on theirs. I told Mrs. Latimoore (J Ellen Axson Elementary school in Jacksonville Florida) that I did not want to leave her class. She was forceful and got me out of the class into regular classes. This beautiful half European and Latino lady had a tremendous impact on my life because of the actions she took on my behalf without the help of my mother. My mother just signed off on whatever she had to keep the school out of business.

I had to give you a background of why I began to look for love in all the wrong places. I am not talking about men either. They were just a tool for me to get what I wanted sexually and financially. I am talking about trying to connect to that one person that I would feel save with, whether it was a friendship with a female old or young or a family member I could count on that would never let me down. This search took place over a period of years. I searched for love and or loyalty from another human from the time my grandfather dies until I was in my late thirties.

As mentioned before, my cousin, who is ten years younger than I, told me I needed to find someone to confide in because I held too much on the inside and one day it was going to make me explode. I choose this woman that kept my son. I paid her on time and well for keeping my son. I did not trust her completely, but I took my cousin's advice that she was more gifted in spirit than I. She said to at least find someone that I could halfway trust and talk with them to let things out, so they do not fester on the inside of me. I had given my life over to Christ but did not know how to live with expressing anger and frustration without physically fighting, cursing someone out or cutting someone. I had also become a mat for people to walk all over me. In my old world, the sinful world I came out of, one would call me weak. All I knew, I wanted to live for Christ. So, I began to have heartfelt talks with this woman. Our relationship developed.

I halfheartedly trusted her with all my personal deep experiences and problems I would have. She would give me advice according to her way of life not according to the word of God. Toward to ending of our relationship and as I grow in the word of God, things happen. I cannot say that things changed in relationship, but God began to deal with me. He told me to ease away from her. I felt a pulling in my spirit to do this and did not know why. She had not done anything that I knew of to me. She had portrayed me once telling the same women she sent to the hospital, that thought she was better than all the other parents; that would not speak to anyone but the babysitter when she walked in to pick up her son, all my personal business that happened between me and my first husband and had the nerve to tell me that she did it because she saw me and this women as sisters. I told her, "You told her what? I asked her how you could see us as sisters when she never spoke to me, or we have never done anything together. She did not answer that. I got over that. The next portrayal was when her old former sister-in-law wanted to have sex with a man and I and my boys were standing in the way of this female Pastor. The female Pastor's abusive husband had died a year prior to me and by two boys (my son & nephew) coming along and needed a place to stay.

Long Suffering & Portrayal

LET US BACK up a minute, my son's father old area he uses to buy drugs in recognized our son and began to harass him, I had to break my lease to move and had nowhere to go so I asked the female Pastor, could I move in with her, and she allowed it. Now, my babysitter and the female Pastor began to talk a lot during my stay at the Pastor's home. These two women had a love and resentment relationship. But now they both had something in common, me. I and my babysitter's relationship ended when she withheld that the Pastor, her former sister-in-law wanted to put me out and locked me out one night and I and my boys: my son and nephew had to come back to her house and wait until the female Pastor she could unlock burglary bars to the door. She admitted that she knew that the Pastor wanted me out of her house. But God! Neither one of them knew that God had already spoken to me and told me I needed to find a place to stay quick, and I did. I shocked the Pastor when one day she sat me down and said she needed to talk to me. She told me that I needed to find me a place to stay and that she gave me two weeks to find one. I told her that I had already found a place that I would be moving to by the end of the week. She was so shocked and stunned that she stumbled on her words. My boys and I moved out by the end of that week. I did not speak or see neither woman for ten years. I would not take my son to see the women that kept him from three months old until elementary school. I developed a relationship with the babysitter that I had changed his school to her address so he could walk home with her other grandchildren, putting her down as his grandmother too and giving her permission to act on my behave. This woman portrayal, I leaned on, loved, and did everything she ever asked me to do hurt me to the core. When I sat back and looked at our relationship, it was always one sided. I gave 100% and she gave the minimum listening ear and uncanny advice. She would never come to my church when I invited her, which meant a great deal to me at that time, but it was required that I attended her church functions. Hang in here on this relationship because later a turn of events will shock you of what took place ten years later.

Family

I TRIED TO lean on my family. I tried to connect with one of my twin sisters to be close too. That did not work because they were close to each other and would tell each other everything. One of the twins I did not trust at all. The other one I trusted with everything but a man. The one I did not trust with a man; went after one of the three men I was seeking at the time. I am the oldest and did not play the childish, young adult games they played with one another: taking each other's boyfriends and sleeping with them too.

I tried to get close to my youngest brother but that did not work out. Five years after my first husband divorced my brother portrayed me twice along with one of the twins' sisters, I never completely trusted. Divorce was a hard one emotionally, but it was a peaceful event from beginning to end. After five years of not talking, seeing, or thinking about this man, my brother next to me in age, died. Everyone assumed that I would become a basket case like I was with Mickey Mouse death my favorite sibling, but they were so wrong. I had grown so much in the Lord,

I was not the same sister, ex-wife, or person anyone knew. I grieved my brother's death in the normal way. Rodney was born after me. We talked off and on and had a healthy relationship. It was so much drama going on with the planning of his funeral. He was separated from his wife a year at that time. She had gone on with her life and my brother too. I talked to my siblings back and forth about what was going on. I sent funds to help bury my brother. My youngest brother gave my ex-husband my number to call without asking my permission. I had just gotten to sleep when I got a call around 7am in the morning from my ex-husband. I thought it was one of my siblings trying to keep me informed so I answered phone. He said hello. I did not recognize the voice. I said, "Who is this?" he said, "your husband." I said no this is not because I am not married." He said, "I am your husband, that's what the bible said." Now this use to be drug dealer is quoting the bible. Nevertheless, I thought he did not know any better and I could not get upset with him because he knows not what he do. I told him according to the word of God; it said let no man put asunder what God has put together and God did not put us together. I then told him that I did not give my number to him and that we had nothing in common and I would ask that he do not call me and hang up the phone. He kept calling me afterwards. He thought like the rest that I would need someone, and he would fill in the gap like he did when my favorite brother, Mickey Mouse died in a car accident about six years before Rodney died. My youngest brother and one of the twins admitted that they had given him my number. My youngest brother told me he had given him my number and told him that he thought I still had feelings for him. I asked my brother, how did he come to that conclusion? I did not ask about him. I have not mentioned his name at any time during our many conversations. My brother went on to say that our family was cursed. I told him, I am not cursed because I belong to God and what God has blessed no man can curse, this is his promise to his children and that he and the twins need to get right with God so they could live better lives. I would not say this is portrayal from my brother, although he knew I was an ordained minister and had been preaching and teaching, but what he did next was the portrayal.

One day me and my neighbor, who practice WICCA was sitting on the front step of my house. **Side note: WICCA is white Witchcraft.** God had sent me into this woman's life to win her back over to where she once was. As we sat on the porch of my house, I was in deep prayer to keep me covered during interactions with her, the anointing fail heavy upon me. Now, I had slight attitude, like what is it now God? Then I repented and said sorry God, what is it? I had to put my hands on Ms. S hand and told her to be quite for a minute; the Lord was trying to tell me something. She silent herself. The spirit of the Lord said look to your right and watch for a while. I looked and said I do not see anything God, then the spirit lifted. We began to talk again. The Spirit moved again on me to be quiet and watch to my right again. I saw a cream white car pass by my street. The spirit lifted again.

Then it fell again as the car slowly turned down my street and rode slowly by my house. The Lord said that is your ex-husband and your brother leaned all the way back in the passenger side of the car. There was tint on the car. I told God cannot be true; my brother would not do such a thing. I would bet my life on this! He would not do something like this. I was in straight up denial. When the car finally rode out of sight, I told my white witchcraft older lady friend that the Lord had showed me that the car that rode by slow in front of my front door was my ex-husband and brother showing him where I lived. She was scared for me, she said Tonya, "You better get into your house and lock the doors. I told Ms. S to go home, and everything was going to be all right. God warned me in the spirit and showed it to me in the natural and tried to talk myself out of believing what I saw because this was my youngest brother. I said the tint was too dark even though I saw the silhouette of my ex-husband's body shape. I know how he sits in his cars, and I saw the silhouette of my brother too. My brother's seat was leaning back as if to almost lay down so I could not see him, but I did. Yet, I still talked myself out of it. When I got into the house the phone rang and guess who it was? My brother had just shown my ex-husband where I lived. I called their bluff and did not answer the phone to say that I was not home or to beat them at their own game. I still was not convinced. While talking to my twin sister's child's grandmother she voluntarily told me that my ex-husband was in Jacksonville the same week this incident happened. I was hurt, crushed, and devastated. I would have bet my life that my brother would not do such a thing and would have lost my life. That was so hurtful. I said this is going to take some time to get over. The first time they gave my ex-husband my number, I changed my number because he kept calling me. I wanted to let him know I did not want to hear from him to the extent to change my number he will get the picture even though people can find out your new number on the internet. I told my living siblings not to give my number out without talking to me first. When my mother died the next year after my brother, they gave my number to my ex-husband again and then my baby brother showed him where I lived. My ex-husband came to Jacksonville for my mother's funeral. One of my siblings invited him. I did not treat him badly. I gave him a minister hug and said thanks for paying his respect to my mother and immediately kept it moving by thanking others from coming. After all this, I began to ponder, I could have a decent friendship with him, and I could win one for the kingdom of God. I did not ask God if I should do this, it was just some thoughts. I did not have any interest in him because I had been transformed into a new person over a five-year period and I was not the same person. I rested. After a couple of days, God gave me a dream that surprised me about my ex-husband. He showed me in the dream that he would try to kill me by one of his female friend's hands. I was riding in the back seat of the car singing and worshipping God, having a good time. He and this female friend sitting up front, him driving and her sitting next to him. I prayed for them in the back seat within myself. God showed me what was going on in the front after a log ride into the woods. He tried to give her a gun to shoot me. I jumped out of the back seat of the car and began running down some high corn fields. He stopped the car and began shooting at me himself after the young lady refuse to take my life for him. When I woke up the next morning, I said thank you Lord for the warning. I will not be making friends with him at all. I began to praise God.

Friendship

ANOTHER PERSON I tried to be close to my roommate. She was the one who went after me to get me into the church and a relationship with God. She made me nervous at first. As mentioned earlier, I was so deep into sin, dating three men at one time. During the time that my first husband was arrested, and I was pregnant with his son, she lived with me. I wanted to be close to her but there was always an invisible spiritual divider there. We began to call each other best friends. Well, the federal government began tapping my phones because my husband at that time and the one I just got through talking about a page or two ago was heavily engaged in some illegal things. The phones would crack, and echo badly. She asked me what was wrong with the phones even though she had discerned what was going on. I told her. I had never done any illegal things. I worked two jobs for about four years to get what I desired, and I was upset about why the feds would be tapping my phones. I told her not to be concerned and assured her that I had never participated in illegal activities but once when I was twelve. When I was twelve, a drug dealer to come into our apartment to set up shop to sell cocaine while my mother had abandoned us in Miami Florida with three babies in pampers and no food for the older three children. He said that my mother had given him permission and that he would not hurt me or allow anyone to touch me. I believed him. At that time my mother, had left town with a younger Haitian man because she had told my violent abusive, heroin using stepfather where we were. I never touched the drug or sold it but allowed someone to come in to sell it. We were so hungry before this man came along. The only thing left we had to eat was a can of government peanut butter with the white and black label. We older children would take turns eating spoons full of peanut butter because that was the only food left to eat. I remember my chubby brother next to me in age left the peanut butter on the kitchen table without the lid on it and a few roaches got into peanut butter. I shook the roaches out of the container. I then scraped the outer parts the roaches feces off. I and my older two siblings ate from that can of government peanut butter again with portioned tabled spoons. It is a wonder that we had not been taken into the foster care system already. I allowed the guy to do this until my mother decided to return, by that time my stepfather had been at the house for about a week, and he was having a good time. He had asked the guy could he sell some drugs for him. I pulled the guy to the side and told him not to do it because he was on heroin, and he would only take the drugs and use it for himself. The guy gave him a package to sale anyway. He got arrested and lost what little he had left of the guy's product. The guy had some guys waiting on his release to beat him up. At that time, I was happy about them wanting to beat him because all year he had beaten my mother, he was finally going to get his.

Getting back on topic, my roommate, best friend, left me hanging. She moved out, to her defense, she had bared a lot. I had gone into deep depression, locking myself in my room, not eating or drinking for days at a time, trying to lose the baby from my husband at that time. She did not call to check on me but twice in the beginning then nothing. I lost the nice town home that I purchased prior to dating my husband at that time. I had worked so hard to get my credit together, buy furniture on layaway, buying items to for two years off my two-job salary so when I moved, I had everything I needed and wanted to be comfortable in my new first home. I soon lost everything because I gave up. God was keeping everything, but I gave up. My truck was repossessed. My mortgage was only $454.00 a month at that time. I walked away from it all. God had sustained me for an entire year without any income coming other than welfare, food stamps and roommate paying what, I was not able to pay. So, losing this friendship really hurt badly for years.

I felt she had abandoned me, that she wanted to enjoy the benefits of our relationship because of what I had. Years later, I accepted that she had experienced many challenges with me and could no longer continue. My progress required removing support. I also came to terms with everyone is human, not perfect and one cannot put that type of trust or dependency in anyone but God. You must love people for who God created them to be and not who you want them to be in your life. You may be wondering did I ever talk to this woman again. I realized that she was also affected by my actions and was unsure how to respond to me. I just talk to her when she wants to talk to me without having any expectations of her. I do feel some deep pain every now and then, but I shake it off and do not allow it to move me. You may be wondering if I talk to my siblings, I do when they want too. Every now and then one may get mad at me because I will not help them out of the financial crisis that they created. I keep my life positive and moving.

Years later, I accepted that she had experienced many challenges with me and could no longer continue. For progress to occur, the support was removed.

Paternal Sister

I ALWAYS WANTED and older sister and I had one from my father from another women. I felt like she felt that I was not good enough to hang in her crowd. Her circle includes educated people, dignitaries, and news broadcasters. Although I discerned this from my sister, I did not allow that to move me to try to develop a relationship with her. I did not get to know her until I was in college and homeless. I was homeless because my crazy ex-boyfriend was stalking me and had broken into my room at my cousin's father's rooming house and took everything and I did not feel safe there anymore. No one offered me any help or protection. It was as if they did not care too much. They did not take it serous. My sister told me I could stay two weeks with her and after that I would have to leave. I understood because I discerned her, I was not educated, I was not of her status, and I did not have any stability in my life other than college and in her mind, she was unsure if I were really going to college and if so, would I complete it. She did not want to have the burden of taking care of me. I understood her along with the gift God gave me to discern people. Nearing the end of the two weeks, my sister reminded me that I had to be gone by a certain time that Friday and I said OK. She never asked me if I had a place to go or if she could help me get a place to live on campus. I left that Friday to go sleep in a nearby apartment complex parking lot on a chilly night. I packed clothes around me to keep warm and prayed to God to find out what would be my next move. I needed to find another place to live during the weekend so that I could make it to college during the week with a bath and other necessities. My sister putting me out did not hurt me, God allowed me to know what she was thinking, and I understood. What hurt me was she would not return my calls when I would call from time to time to just stay connected. There were other things that took place that made me give up developing a relationship with my sister over the years. I told God she does not want me; I do not need her. Our biological father worked on me to try to talk to her and I would not. I informed our father about my efforts over the years and the outcomes and conveyed that I will no longer continue to try or hope. God stepped in and gave me a dream. When God showed me the dream, I told God I was willing to take a chance again only because He wanted me too. My sister and I met at a restaurant. She had on the same clothing in the dream God showed the day we met at the restaurant, and I shared that dream with her. God later developed in me to love people as He would love them. In other words, love them where they are at in life and do not love beyond oneself. I used to love deeply and get hurt when I was betrayed or let down. I wear people as loose garments but love and be concerned about them in a healthy way.

Church Folk & Witchcraft

THE FIRST TIME I entered a church that I can recall was at age eleven. My beloved Aunt had just got saved as they would call it. Before my aunt wore hot pants, drank beer, and got into it with her husband every Friday or Saturday night. Despite her demeanor on Friday and Saturday towards her husband, she was very loving. She loved to feed people. The first thing she would do when you came to her house was to hug and kiss you, Yuck! She would then ask you, "are you hungry? My mother never had any sisters; she was the only girl amongst male siblings. My mother married my favorite Aunt "X," only favorite brother. As mentioned prior, this man spent most of his young adult life in prison, he used heroin by needles, and he beat the Hell out of my mother when he was high and out of his mind. The drug altered his personality altogether. He was like a raging demon out of control and not knowing what he would do next to cause brutality upon my mother. As mentioned prior, as a child I would talk my mother into leaving this man before he killed her, and he would always charm her into staying with him.

My favorite aunt "X" lived far out in the country part of Jacksonville when I was eleven. A local church in the country would ride through the country area going door to door to get people to come to their church preaching Hell is real and one needed to decide where they wanted to spend eternity. On few occasions, members of the church visited, but my aunt chose to hide in her trailer to avoid interaction. Eventually, she embraced the faith, but her husband remained unconvinced. When I joined this family, my aunt was someone I was beginning to get to know. However, before I could learn more about her previous lifestyle, she converted to a new faith. Her personality totally changed as if she had been through a cult. It appeared her personality changed overnight. She dressed differently and wanted everyone else to dress modestly as she did. She did not want people to say curse words or swear words around her. Everyone thought she had lost her mind. I did not think she was crazy. She looked so different. She looked peaceful and beautiful. I thought to myself whatever she found, I wanted some of that. I did not think of the church folk, I thought that whatever she experienced it was beyond church and people. To me she was an angel on earth.

After my aunt had grown a little in the word of God and how to minister specifically to the sinner man, she finally got my mother to go to church with her and bring us kids. When I walked in, I felt comfortable at first and began to observe. I kept quiet. As mentioned before, children were expected to be silent. If someone was uncertain about the situation and felt uneasy, it was prudent to wait until their parents were at ease and attentive before asking questions that persisted in their mind. In frequent times, even then, they did not give you an answer and you felt that it was not your business or that you did not need to know. Grown-ups would often say that is not your concern or why you want to know that and if it were something they felt that they did not want to answer, they would say wait until you are grown, you will understand than or my favorite just keep on living you will know by and by. Funny, at that time of childhood none of these saying made any sense to me and to me, it was grown-ups' way of saying I do not want to answer your questions, and I do not owe you an explanation. Children were expected to listen, obey, and refrain from questioning adults. It would cost you a "Jap slap" dead in your mouth. It only took one time to get "Jap Slapped" because they would hit you so hard that the pain would ring in your lips, and you will feel your inner lip sting and you would check your teeth to see if they were all still there. Now day's children talk along with adults in adult conversation, and they will stand up to you as if they are your equal and could only be five years old. No home training as they would say.

As the service got off the grown in the church. I looked and saw how they carried on and called on Jesus as if he were deaf. They said they called this the Holy Spirit. One had to call him for a long, long, long time. The person would be at alter on their knees or laying on the floor until someone deemed that they had received the Holy Spirit. I thought to myself an eleven-year-old is it the holy spirit that come upon them or a demon or an induced an altered state of mind through repetitious words and exhaustion for some reason Is this was a form of ignorance, that they had made this up to wear out people until they submitted to the control of whoever the leader was. If you did not follow what the leader said, you were rebellious or you had a demon inside of you and you needed deliverance. **It was a laughable scene.** On the other hand, as a child I could see that something was not right with a person's spirit but to label everyone that think the way you want them too or do things the traditional way to called them rebellious or demon controlled, possessed was a bit much. In many of these traditional beliefs in churches, like the one I am describing, witchcraft is heavily practiced.

I consider one form of witchcraft in ministry is the controlling factor by trying to brainwash people into submission to the Pastor or leader. Jesus was a gentleman. He did not produce all kinds of sermons to push people into following a human man. A true leader or Pastor of Jesus Christ would point people solely to God and not gimmicks such as follow the Pastor vision; Helped the pastor with his vision and in due Season you will have your own vision. It is my opinion that Jesus said to take the Gospel to throughout the world. The bible talks about discipleship and sitting under a shepherd to learn how to live in this world as a new creature, how to fight temptations that causes one to do things that makes one sick to the stomach that is not pure. All creatures were born with an instinct of right and wrong and by a certain age they knew the difference.

Getting back to this calling on the holy spirit. One do not have to beg the holy spirit if one has confessed their wrongs, believe Jesus died for all of our sins and arose to ascend into heaven, that he sits on the right hand of God and asked Jesus to come into their heart (Ephesians 1:13, John 14:26 of the Bible, Kings James

Version). The comforter is immediately sent to one as a gift of protection, guide, teacher or whatever you need Him to be in your walk as a new creature in Jesus Christ. Another weird thing about what this ministry did was one's appearance had to be plain, almost Quaker like: long dresses that came down to your ankles, no hair dyes, no make-up at all, light pasty stockings. Funny, one time my mother dyed her hair and mind. She had just got into seeking God. My beloved aunt told her that her hair looked like to pits of Hell and that she needed to dye her hair back black and mind. I was hot, I thought I looked different, it boosted my low self-esteem. I felt empowered but not to the point in talking back or disrespecting any adult. My mother listens to my beloved aunt and dyes both of our hair back to black. I still loved my aunt dearly, but I knew she was wrong about this, and I knew she was brain washed in the areas of how one should live their life (appearance plain). I guess Queen Ester in the bible being prepared for months before going before the King, was just one detailed my aunt and her ministry interpret differently. Weird hah?

Speeding ahead, over the years, I highly esteemed this aunt still even though I did not agree with all that she was brain washed to believe by her ministry leaders. My aunt and her relationship with her sinner husband were crazy to me. She had gotten saved as they would say and became this woman that had to do everything her sinner husband told her. He could talk to her in any kind of way and do her any kind of way. They were taught to pray for their spouse. She pounded this into my mother head just like her brother pounded on my mother and almost killed my mother. My favorite aunt's husband would call her stupid and dumb on the regular. She would say, well honey what would you have me do? He would say sometimes "get out of my way, what you doing does not make no damn sense." Sometimes he would say, "X," where your head is because you ain't using it, a mind is a terrible thing to waste. I watched my beloved aunt verbally abused for years by her husband. The traditional church had brainwashed her to believe she had to put up with her husband's mental abuse. Yes, he was an exceptionally good provider and was not a whorish man she would always point out. She felt like she had a good man although he talked to her like she was a mentally challenged individual. He was a very thrifty man putting it very mildly. He believed in recycling all kinds of items and brainwashed her by doing abnormal things to save money too. She was a stay-at-home spouse. My beloved aunt stayed home and cleaned, cooked, and made sure she completed everything her husband told her to do. When he got home, he would talk to my aunt as if he were talking to a two-year-old child, he would ask if she did this and if she done that.

As a child I always observed and pondered on the idiotic things that adults would do or let happen. I would say to myself with strong conviction, when I group, up I am never doing that, that did not make sense what those grown adults did. I would also say that I was not putting up with a man beating on me or talking to me the way my favorite aunt "X husband did her. I thought of all kinds of ways of putting a man out of his misery for talking to me like my favorite aunt "X" husband did her.

Fast speed ahead again, in the years to come, as an adult I got close to both my aunt and uncle. My uncle had finally surrender to God after twenty plus years of marriage and degrading my aunt. A scripture comes to mind: Beloved I wish above all things that you prosper as your soul prospers. We make choices in life. God gave us the ability to make choices and allows us to experience the consequence of our choices. Getting back to my relationship with this couple. For years I would take care of their personal letters of business. I would check on them and my only tie to them was long relationship after my mother finally divorced this animal of a man, brother of this beloved aunt. My younger brother and sisters were related to my beloved aunt and uncle by blood. My brother and sisters did not even call our aunt and uncle to ask how they were doing or just to talk to them. They raised them from toddlers up to pre-teens before my aunt would allow my mother to take them back. She made my mother promise she would take good care of them and do not allow any hurt or harm to come to my younger three siblings. How could they not keep track of this elderly couple that has been there for them whether they were right or wrong? At any rate, I had gotten over that fact that my favorite aunt almost cost me my walk with Jesus Christ years earlier (She told me, I had to first receive the Holy spirit. This was her response when I mustered up the courage to finally tell her I had gotten saved. Remember, her ministry believed in tarrying or begging to receive the Holy Spirit?)

I called tarrying or begging for something God already gave you. A person that becomes a believer may not feel an anointing because one has not studied the word of God with the help of the Holy Spirit. You must build up your spiritual strength in God with reading his word (The Christian bible) and praying.

I would go over to my beloved aunt and uncle's house at least once or twice a month to check on them to make sure that it was not something I could do for them that they needed done. I desire to take care of them and that they would not have to worry about bills, medical and any other necessities. My heart ached to provide for them. You may be wondering about the years of mental abuse my aunt suffered in a marriage with my uncle? Why would I want to help him? One word: forgiveness and my aunt were more at peace, and she stilled loved this man. Who can go up against that? He also had tone down his harsh words to her. He would start out saying something and catch himself and just be boiling but would shut his mouth. Physically he would get up and start doing what she could not do how he wanted her to do it. I learn later in life also while in my mid-thirties that these women had choices not to stay in the state, they were in with these men, but they choose tolerate for whatever reason. My mother had too many children, six and who was going to want her with six kids, which is what my stepfather drilled in her head. I do not know what did it was for his sister to stay with her husband all those severe mentally abusive years? One thing I believe in, a Pastor/Warlock would always say, "Just because someone call you something, it does not mean you are that. You can be whatever you want to be if you want it that bad."

Spiritual Birth

WHEN I FIRST got "saved" as they would say (I personally call it converted because there was a great change in the following areas: emotionally, spiritually, and the physical changed as well). I was riding down by Jacksonville College in my nice burnt orange; Ford Explore truck that had a tan leather interior. I was wearing a short but professional cream white attire on, Maybelline mascara in place, lipstick and makeup looking lovely. I did not have any music on. I always loved quiet times (no noise from any electronic device) either early in the morning or late in the evening. Mind clear as a bell. I went to thinking, God I am tired of the same old. I go to different clubs from time to time to party. I see a pattern, where I will not go to a club for six months and then go to a new club, and see the same people at that new spot, doing the same old thing and they are aging but still acting as if they are fresh out of college. Boring, I told God that I want a new life God, I have tried many things in life. I have done a few things that I say I would never do. I have had a great time partying and experiencing different atmosphere of people in all levels of society, and nothing is stimulating me anymore. Lord, I have tried everything I was big and bad enough to try, God I want to try you. I began to say, Lord I have done a lot of wrongs, and I ask you to come into my heart and live. Lord washes me whiter than snow. Instantly, things began to change. I began to cry while driving to work. By the time I got to work, Maybelline black mascara was everywhere. I stepped out of my truck, my body felt super clean inside out, my body was not the same. I looked up at the sky, it was super bright, the trees were the prettiest green I had ever seen in my life, everything was super bright. I got back into my truck and began to get my face together before I walked into work. I was a new creature. By that afternoon, I asked God to help me stay this way, that I do not know how to maintain this walk and that I need major help. Me with a four-year degree, a leader in every job I had taken. At that point I was acting like a child and did not know how to make decision about how I should live my life and asking for God, the Holy Spirit and Jesus to keep me. Say what you want, I did not know how to live Godly. I did not want to lose that relationship with God. My life was always missing something before I allowed God to come into my heart. When he entered, I felt whole. The search was over. I did not even know I was searching for aimlessness until something spoke through me to let me know I was not happy and reminded me I was a complete being. Something was missing. To God be the glory! For the great things he had done in my life.

Baby on Milk Spiritually

ATTENDING CHURCH SERVICE was challenging at times because I observed others expressing their gratitude to God with phrases like "Thank you Jesus," "Praise God," and "Hallelujah." I used to wonder why I couldn't be saved like that." Instead, I would praise God inwardly. Later I discovered praising and worshipping him inwardly was just as good and precious as the outward verbal display. As time went on, I grew in the knowledge of God. What does that mean? It means that I read my bible but did not understand all that I read but as time passed and I sat under leaders that taught the bible and I would go home to re-read and make sure they use the scriptures correctly or they use it to explain something. Sometimes leaders use the scriptures in a separate way than they meant. I liked leaders who told people up front that they use a particular scripture different than what it meant to get their personal attention to something the Spirit, Holy Ghost wanted to open their eyes too, to correct and/or bring knowledge to them. **The more I studied and were around imperfect people, the more I grew spiritually.**

Experiences That Grew Me Stronger

FUNNY, WHEN I was a sinner (not in a covenant relationship with God, meaning did not invite him in my life/heart to take control. I talked to him occasionally and when I was in a jam; like Jeannie in a bottle). As a child I talked to him all day. He was my imaginary friend. No that I became a young adult; I was a bad ass. After being defenseless against my stepfather beating on my mother when he gets frustrated or doped up, I promise myself "ain't no one going to take advantage of me or treat me any kind of way." I respect people and they are going to respect me, or I will beat them down. I came over to The Lord's side and became a wimp! My personal conception and what church folks had taught me was to turn the other cheek and keep turning. Imagine being constantly verbally and mentally abused and not taking actions. One only prays. Imagine coming from a very violent background as a child and growing up into adolescents in violence and loved ones taking actions against those who wrong them how they see fit. This sat my spiritual mind in a spin. My stomach would be turning upside down when someone lies on me for no cause, takes something that was mind and totally disrespect me in any manner. My insides would churn, in my mind I was in turmoil not reacting to my natural instincts: beat them down, then I would feel better and most of the time I did. Instead, mentally, and spiritually, I would cry deeply. God, himself brought deliverance: He taught me through the Holy Spirit. After going through what people were doing to me on the inside of the church as well as outside of the church, people stepping all over me and I allowing it. The holy Spirit told me enough, "God did not save you for you to become a wimp on his side but a warrior." The words of God that people of God told me to turn the other cheek did not explain the concept in the spiritual sense that I could understand.

What they should have said "allow the spirit of Christ within you to speak for you when you are attacked." Mature believers know to stay calm while under an attack. They know how to humble themselves so the Holy Spirit increases. They know that the Holy Spirit will speak of something that would make a savage, raging lunatic come to a halt. When I got this great revelation, it brought so much peace to my mental turmoil during times of people lying, cheating me, and taking from me and even disrespecting me by yelling at me for no apparent reason other than they messed up and wanted to use me as a whipping board. It was on, The Holy Spirit kept cutting down my aggressors. I was totally amazed at times by what the Holy Spirit was saying through my fleshly mouth. I was like the cheerleader later, thinking Wow you go Holy Spirit, you are a bad man. You handled, that, I would have never thought of saying something as profound and skillful as what you said, Holy Spirit. I took my trust to another level by asking the Holy Spirit to oversee protecting me from all hurt and harm and including myself. Sometimes we can make bad choices in life financially, relationships and just want what we want when we want it. It may not be the time for you to get certain things but a few of us will do all that it takes and take crazy risks to get what we want, and the timing is bad. I trusted the Holy Spirit with what I asked him. Therefore, I did not have to have mental walls up with people. My guards were down to the Holy Spirit to protect me, warn me of dangers and many other things, such as teaching me things in the spirit I was ready to handle when I grew up.

More Experiences That Grow Me

I HAVE MENTIONED some relationships in earlier chapters that were also a part of my spiritual growing in the Lord although they were some horrific situations. Earlier I covered my first marriage as a baby believer and an older woman that portrayed me deeply (I had picked her as the one to confide in and she told all my personal business to another female parent that thought she was better than any of the other female parents that came through the woman's house to retrieve their child or children). Moving on, I moved to Dunn Avenue side of town after my first divorce. This was the second darkest experience as a believer I lived through. I lost everything, and my family did not support me but criticized me instead. My mother taught me to be self-reliant rather than ask for help. I knew how to survive. When I first moved into the apartment outside Dunn Avenue side of Jacksonville Florida, there was a heaviness I felt when I entered the apartment, but I could not understand why until later. I had my pastor at that time to come in and pray over the place. One may say later I had a double dose of a curse in my dwelling. I experienced so many mental anguishes in that apartment that it no wonder, I did not lose my mind. I had people in the apartment complex that did all kinds of wicked things outside of my apartment. One time I found two eggs thrown on the back of my patio: they looked as if they were still on the inside, intact of the eggshell. The yoke did not run into the whites of the egg and the whites of the egg did not run into the yellow part of egg. God had already warned me in not so specific way but when I saw that, a little fear entered my heart. I had never seen anything like that in my life, and it was highly unlikely that throwing an egg that it did not run and mixed with white and yellow. I left the ministry that the pastor that had blessed my apartment and went to another ministry to learn more about conducting ministry in an orderly fashion.

My heart desires to learn more about running a ministry in a Godly order. After that, my finances suffered badly. I was tithing, sowing into the new ministry by making baskets, traveling with the Pastors, and serving them faithfully. I was a single mother of my son and nephew with no assistance from others. I worked a full-time job at the Internal Revenue Service, which served as my daytime Hell hole. The book of Job mentions that he had no peace during the day (IRS), nor when he slept (occasional terrifying dreams). This was surely me, suffering mentally. I had so many people that envied me that I was not aware until years later. I did not understand this. I was quiet, it did not bother anyone.

Did not gossip or do clicks. I was helpful to those I needed to be or moved to be. When I began my spiritual journey, I asked God to teach me more about Himself. I wanted to know all it was to know about my God, the son, and the Holy Spirit. Well, He chose patient and longsuffering at the Internal Revenue Service. I hated the job at IRS from day one of training and continued into my third year. I cried almost every day up until the second and third year of working at IRS. I hated the job so much. I applied to so many other agencies that deal with foster care. I always had a good name as an overachiever at whatever job I held. Look at the picture, I am a single parent of two male young boys living in a high crime apartment area where the police had their yellow crime tape roped off around my door almost every Thursday and Friday evening, my boys could not go outside to play, my son's father had bought drugs from that area and they knew my son and asked him about his father, I left one church because the man I held as a father figure kissed me in the mouth prior to a program God had given me to do, went to another church where, I had to try to earn their trust. Witchcraft and voodoo are targeting my finances and mind. I would go without eating for days at a time to ensure my boys had enough food to eat until payday. I would go around to the coffee area of IRS and load up on coffee to curb my appetite. Sometimes people that I trusted to eat from would bring me something to eat unexpectedly and I would thank God within and them verbally. I never mentioned to them that I was starving or was weak and needed to eat. I recall another incident that I experienced that I will never forget as long as I live when I went to Publix Grocery Store on the Dunn Avenue side of Jacksonville Florida. I prayed deeply as I drove to the store. I have $5.00 to buy food to last my boys 3 days until payday. I had enough gas in my car to last me until payday. I went into Publix and bought a three-course meal that consisted of one meat and sides. I do not remember the side items, but it was a balanced, average American meal. I remember after day three, my son noticed I was not eating and said he did not want anymore that I needed to eat what he left. I told him no that he must eat to be able to focus on school the next day. This was just one darkest time in my life.

Summary of Darkest Time in My Life

(**AS AN ADULT**, so far, I have had three darkest times: 1. was living off Dunn Avenue, Hart's Road. The church folks. Car repossession (having to walk with two young boys down the long winding road of Harts Road to bus stop), getting a donated fixer upper car, that as soon as I got it the alternator and the starter went bad on it, the IRS job and divorce. 2: Lost everything within a month's time (lovely townhome in a beautiful neighborhood) a vehicle, furnisher. Became homeless for the second time. The first time was when I was hiding from a boyfriend that stalked me (my sister allowed me to stay two weeks with her, then I had to go and left with nowhere to go. Spent two nights sleeping in my car. On the third day, I was allowed to exit the IRS indefinitely. Once again everyone that I held very dear and close to my heart turned their backs on me.)

More Darkness in Relationships

MY MOTHER IN the Lord at that time asked me why in Hell did I walk off my IRS job. I do not remember all the deeply hurtful things this woman said to me and do not care to remember. This woman caused me to cry for a week as if I had lost my best friend as I did years earlier. I never experienced such mental pain as this person caused me in my time of distress. There is a time and place for everything. If a person makes a poor choice or if you think it is a life changing decision, never kick a person when they are down. That is not the end of their story. The first two events mention almost cost me my mind. The third event, I was stronger. God had brought me through too much and saved my life from many things to insult my God by turning my back on him. I was deeply hurt by the person I loved most, besides my son. I knew I would get over this pain and move on. It was just allowing it to take its course and wade through the process of breaking down and then building back up. I only had a handful of people I allowed in my front seat of my life. Everyone that I held close to me either walked away or drove the steak deep into my heart for God to have me to let them go. After all, the spirit of the Holy Spirit told me, that "no man is going to get the credit for what I am going to do in your life." Funny, I had an Ike and Tina Turner type of relationship with the two woman that were the closet to my heart. I had promised myself that people are people and that no matter what they do, say or act toward me, I will stick with them. Sometimes we do not know what we should pray for as we ought, but the Holy Spirit makes intercessions for us groaning and utterings that cannot be explained. I am healed of that and still love these people as God does.

I was always down sick periodically where at times I could not get out of my bed or even lift my head off my pillow. I recall one incident, where my four-year-old nephew I taught how to pray and read a few words of the bible came into my bedroom of this double cursed dwelling. (I say double cursed because years later God revealed to me that my fatherly pastor that I had asked to bless my apartment that had kissed me in the mouth, which had sent unclean spirits to torment me was in fact a Warlock.) My nephew came into my room and said, "Momma, are you all, right? I said, "No." I could not raise my head to even look at him. He then said, "Do you want me to pray for you? I said yes and wondered how he was going to get to me in this extremely high bed I adored so. My nephew climbed up pole like he was experienced, then crawled his way speedily toward my head in the bed, he laid his little hand over my forehead and began to pray two words, then spoke in tongues. I was shocked that he created a powerful prayer that brought deliverance to me. Within just thirty minutes I was fully recovered and got out of my bed of afflictions to fix breakfast for my boys. Whether my four-year-old nephew pretended to speak in tongues, the concern and sincerity of the prayer brought deliverance from what had me bound at that time. I will never forget this as long as I live. I should have lost my mind. What kept me? Reading my bible during hard the times and when I was at my lowest point of almost giving up. The 30 days, 45 days, even 60 days fasting I went on to stay strong kept me as well. Or maybe it was a combination of both reading, meditating on scriptures to get me through the day at the Hell hole of IRS and a double cursed dwelling place at night. I should have lost my mind but God's Grace's.

Working in the New Ministry

IN THE MINISTRY of the new church, I became a part of a new adventure that afforded the opportunity to experience a lot of negative not much positivity believes. Some existing members expressed concern regarding the rapid assignment of my position upon joining the ministry. I was in the position of minister in this ministry, but I was on a two-year probationary trail for them to watch my character. So, I was only allowed to wear a tap collar instead of a full collar in which I was ordained a few years prior to this ministry for by a different ministry? I went by their rules, it did not matter, I just wanted to help these, Pastors. I also was a private intercessor for this ministry and two other ministries. I would sometimes be up half the night praying for the Pastors of my new church and the two other ministries. I would intercede while my male Pastor preached. The purpose was to help him stay on tract of what God gave him to preach; to let God use him to give the congregations their daily Sunday bread to last them until they get back to the Church (The House of prayer). The male and dominant Pastor had this cliché he uses to always mention sometimes several times when he would bring the word: "Hurting people hurt people." Later God revealed to me that this Pastor was still hurting on what happen to him in his last ministry and a previous marriage that ended badly. The dominant male Pastor would sometimes mention every now and then in front of the whole church that he does not put his trust in no man and that just because Minister Artis is the minister of the house, he still must watch me. I was a little put out when he first said such a thing. I spoke to God inwardly, saying God I am faithful, why would he say embarrassing statement like that in front of the whole church. My feelings were so hurt but I still obeyed my Pastors, served them faithfully and did not run and talk to anyone else about them. What I experienced and knew spiritually, I kept to myself and prayed for them both. On one occasion of serving, the dominant male Pastor was in his office and had taken apart a picture that his other members convinced him to put up in the church during the church's anniversary celebration. Unfortunately, the task was assigned to me. I was not happy about it at all because he had told the church that he did not like pictures of the Pastors up in churches. I wanted to comply with his decision that he did not want his or his or his wife's picture up in the church. When I saw Pastor sitting in his office and had disassembled the photo, I was severely hurt. My mind went to spinning, why would Pastor think I would try to do anything wicked to him? Pastor is from a place that witchcraft was practice as a way of life, but he should be led by the spirit of Christ and not his flesh. I was hurt. I had taken a lot of things, but I had to talk to both Husband and wife to let them know how I felt. I am a straightforward person, and I pick my battle. I had allowed a lot of things to be said to me without arguing or disrespecting my leaders. I had overlooked quite a few things. When I had stopped hurting so much, I asked to have a private meeting with both. I told them that I had seen where someone had taken apart the picture that I was assigned to put together, that I had took my time to make sure it was straight and no particles were on inside of glass to see it was disassembled made me think that my Pastors thought I was working witchcraft or voodoo on them severely hurt my heart because I would not even do such a thing to my worst enemy because of my love of God. Witchcraft, black magic, voodoo, anything that is opposite of God was not of him and I do not do such things. The Pastors did not even respond to my question or provide an explanation. They would not even address how I felt, they only said that I needed some rest. I looked at them and said yes, you are right; I need some rest. I laughed within myself and said God, I thank you, and the devil is a liar. I looked at them one last time before I left their office to show them how disappointed I was in them. What I assumed of them was true from their avoidance of my questions. After this encounter, I had to go to God and ask him to heal my deep hurt from this and I trusted and believed that he would, and he did.

Another incident that occurred at this ministry was when the whole church traveled out of town to a convention. I have always treasured my quiet time with the Lord alone. Well, my Pastors demanded that I stay in the room with the other female women, which was uncomfortable for me. I told my Pastors, that I did not want to because I was not a morning person that my mind was only up to God first thing in the morning, that I had to have my quiet time with the Lord. I was used to being alone in prayer in the morning and I did not interact with anyone early in the morning, my boys did not interrupt my prayer time. They insisted and what I discovered in that conversation was that they needed me to keep a watch over the women in which it made me more uncomfortable, and it was disrespectful. These were grown women. I prayed and stayed in the room with ladies, but I did not spy on them, it was not of God to me. One of the ladies battled with her sexuality. She was attracted to women and that made me uncomfortable. I had been celibate for ten years at that time, and I did not talk about men with anyone. I was focus on me and my relationship with God. He healed me of the divorce. I was so enjoying my relationship with God. I was intimate with God, read my bible, had prophetic dreams and open eye visions (open eye visions is when God shows you something within minutes, that if you were sleep it would take you hours to dream it). In this ministry, I concealed my gifts because I was not authorized to use them, and it did not matter if they utilized me for this. I just wanted to serve where I was needed. Getting back to the bi-sexual female, even though I was uncomfortable being around her, she was my protector during this conference. This is why one cannot miss-treat anyone that does not act the way you do or believe what you believe. You never know if that person's is the very one that helps you or defends you when no one else would even though their thoughts towards you at times are not pure or of God. As one can imagine, I was very exhausted from helping my pastors prepare for trip, working, single parent of two male young male boys and being taught long suffering and patient in the Hell Hole of IRS trenches. I had to grocery shopping for my pastor's drinks, mints, and other items they requested I get and have everything ready, have my boys packed up and ready for babysitter. I had to save up to be able to pay for extra hours of care for my boys. I went on trip with about $30.00 dollars or less to spend. I am nervous about that. By the time, the first night got off I was so tired that I could barely keep my eyes open much less watch and pray during service. The young lady that was bisexual was playing an instrument up front near pulpit, so she could see all that was going on. When my female, less dominant pastor got up to speak, there was a problem with the microform. It kept cracking and going out while she spoke and this was a great pet peeve of our dominant male pastor, her husband. He had trained me to take action trying not to distract the speaker, and he made it clear I was to do what I needed to do to clear up problem quickly. So, I did what I was trained to do. When I did, the two Pastors that had somehow connected themselves to our pastor's evil eyed me down. If looks could kill, I would have been beheaded, chopped up in tiny pieces and cremated. When I had cleared up problems and stepped out of the way, I caught a glimpse of their distained for me. Both Male and Female pastors of their own ministry had looked at so harshly.

The bi-sexual member that had played an instrument up front caught those pastors looking at me so badly and saw the hurtful look on my face when I unexpectantly caught their evil glares. She was angry. After another hour of trying to keep my eyes open, I told my pastor, I had to go to lay down before I fall out and that I will be on time and on post faithfully the next morning and I was. When I got up, apparently, the young lady had told the other ladies what she witness happened to me. All of the women were mad, and they had already come to me and told me to talk to our pastors that they did not trust the new relationships with these pastors, and they did not like the fact that those pastors were always given money by our pastors when they needed funds themselves. The members felt that our pastors were being taken advantage of. I told everyone it was not going to last long to pray for our pastors that I could not go to them and tell them such a thing against those pastors. I was not scared but I knew telling them would be ignored because they were so into them. I did not tell the members this, just told them to pray and prayer will take care of it. I had to keep the ladies calm because they wanted to address the issues with those pastors. I asked them not too, to let it be. The young lady that witnesses it was still angry and wanted to confront them and get them straight. It took a long time to convince her not to take action.

When it came for me take a temporary leave this ministry, God had taken me out twice for me to pray and seek his face and to get cleaned up (I was clogged with the traditional religious status of church). I did it in decently and order by going to my pastors and sitting down talking to them that I would be gone for a month. The dominant male pastor told me that I was not following the word because I was forsaking myself to assemble with the believers. God had prepared me for that. I told my dominant male pastor that I would have strong believers around me outside of ministry that I already had covenant relationships with that we Afton challenge one another and have private studies with one another. I went on to tell him that I am not backing away from every believer but needed time to rest, pray, and regroup. He was not happy, but he said, ok. I told them I would be back in a month if they still have me, that I would schedule a meeting with them to see what they would do with me. In the month, God cleanse me of traditionalism, man sub servitude and other things that had invaded my thought life that I could not focus on my own personal relationship with God. I still had meaningful bible studies with other believers over the phone and at work. I did not even know it; God was trying to deliver me out of the ministry because the pastors were too young and inexperienced in the spiritual things of God. When I came back, my gifts increased the more. The Holy Spirit taught me how to manage Godly order. I had dreams and visions and could interpret them. Again, I was not released in this ministry to operate in my gifting, God is not a God of confusions. Many said that I should do what God called me to do no matter what. The Holy Spirit showed me differently; he had me look up scripture and open my understanding to it. The scripture dealt with a prophet is subjected to the pastor. In other words, you go to the pastor for permission before speaking to his flock. Another scripture the Holy Spirit gave me was, your gift will make room for itself. If God wants you to do something, despite the circumstances he will make it impossible for you not to do what he called you to do. This happens once in this ministry. I accompanied both my pastors out of town but early the morning of trip, when my foot hit the floor, God gave me a message for the pastor of the ministry we were going to visit. I told God, how? I was not released/given permission to operate in this area. My pastors did not even know I was an expert in this area prior to coming to their ministry.

I learn early to hide because I did not like being up front in ministry and I did not want anyone to know how God operates through me because in the past others had gotten jealous when God uses me. The Holy Spirit would not give me no peace on the message I had for the Pastor of the ministry we were going to visit; he kept reminding me even after I would try to forget message. At that ministry we had a good time. The last day, as I was walking to the rest room which was in the same direction of the pastor of that church office was, her close armor bearer told me to come that I needed to see her pastor and I said no. She insisted that I needed to see her pastor, so the Holy Spirit reminded me that I had to give the prophecy, so I went in and told her no more than the Holy Spirit told me. Funny, the prophecy was about the same person that insisted that I needed to see her pastor. That pastor had just gotten married to a man and her armor bearer had a secret love for her of which she was not even aware. God revealed this to her, and I had to pray for her because I knew this would hurt her deeply and that she would have to make a difficult decision about this woman. When this pastor came to our ministry to visit, it was evident that my pastors had bad mouthed me because the women did not look in my directions and avoided me like the plaque. God told me to get close enough to her that no one could tell we were speaking and confirm with her what God had use me to tell her. She said it was just what God told you. When we spoke, our heads were turn in other directions so that no one would have thought we even exchanged words. At that point, the poor pastor did not know who to trust because of that uncovering of her armor bearer's secret love for her. I prayed for a week for this pastor, for God to give her a strong defense and discernment to protect her from the sheep in wolves clothing. She did not know who to trust.

During the end of me leaving this ministry, God was giving me dreams back to-back and I would share them with the dominant male pastor in the company of his wife pastor out of respect. I gave him the interpretation of the dreams for various members of church. I asked God if he did not tell the members, to send someone behind me to minister to that person and I believed God did. The wife began to pray for God to give her husband more dreams and visions very heavily. The Holy Spirit always prompts me in when I need to pay attention to someone. Remember, I had trusted the Holy Spirit to protect me, warn me, educate me and anything else that would add to my life. I was preached to in an indirect way(criticize), that I was used to laying on hands, casting out spirits and so forth. Pastor would look my way. I did not even know, the Holy Spirit had to almost knock me down to hip me that the pastor was talking about me. I would always think and say to the Spirit no he is not talking about me; I have not done anything for him to say such things. God delivered out of this ministry because the pastor himself was wounded and not healed and was hurting others, but he was not aware of it. He had followed the advice of other ministries to teach members to obey him. I remember one sermon, I know he got from another ministry, how dumb sheep were, and he used it to cross reference the members as sheep. Sheep (church members) needed directions and to be basically told what to do. In other words, brain washing into doing whatever the pastor said and not having a brain or personally relationship with God to hear from God themselves. I did not want to leave. After all I was a church junkie. I needed to be at the church to help with something. I do not hold any unforgiveness toward any of the ministries God has allowed me to be a part of. Why should I? If I have the love of Christ in me. What profit is it to me if I have the pure love of God and the kingdom of God? I prayed for the ministry that the warlock was over. I did not want him to go to Hell. He still has a chance to be delivered. The pastor that was from the area that witchcraft, voodoo, black magic was prevalent who was deeply wound and not healed, trying to find what works for him by going by the warped directions of other pastors that seek to control their members into doing anything they wanted them to do. He needed pray and I prayed for him and his beautiful wife. The warning God gave me just in case I went back into this ministry was: If I go back to this ministry, I will die a slow spiritual death and allow me to feel a slight feeling of the death I would experience. I could not take it. I cried out God! Please. He lifted the feeling immediately. To drive it home to me, the Church Junky, he showed me the deadliest snake, the mamba snake, his head is shaped like a coven and the inside of his mouth was dark purple. God knows what he be doing to get my attention. A snake gets my attention every time but the deadliest snake, mamba, scared the hell out of me. I said Yes Sir! God knew that I would eventually think about going back to the familiar, what was comfortable to me even though I knew I was not to go back. I would talk myself into going back to a place God brought me out. I do not mean to portray this ministry in a negative way. It is all about my personal walk with God dealt with me individually concerning what he was doing in my life.

Homelessness Again

PRIOR TO LEAVING this ministry, things got worse at the apartment. The men that had sold drugs to my son's father began to harass my son about his father and ask questions about me. From that time on, I did not allow my son to go outside, not even to front door. I had to leave that place. I packed up everything and moved my items to a storage room. My boys and I went to a hotel room for the night. I only had enough money to stay one night at the hotel and gas money to last me until my next pay day at IRS. I met a beautiful, classy, Christian, educated lady. She asked me to move in with her. I had a prophecy from my younger cousin that a pretty, faced woman was going to ask me to move in with her but do not because she does not like to pay her bills. It was much more to be aware of than just that. I did not think God was talking about her. After all she had a higher degree than me and she taught others in the ministry. I moved in with her because I had nowhere to go and no money. While staying with her our spirits did not gel. I was so distraught by what was going on at the apartment that I could not put a finger on what I was feeling. I paid her rent and bought items needed for the household. She visited my ministry and saw that I worked close to my pastors and was very curious of how I got that close to the pastors. She was not in the position she desired at her church at the time and talked about what she wanted to do and wanted to meet with her pastor to express what she wanted to do in the ministry at that time. Her Pastor was a decorated general in the deep spiritual things of God and the ministry world. He had been on TBN, world known Christian channel. He had experienced spiritual things early in ministry that most experienced pastors had not. His own congregation was not ready to receive the deep things God had poured into him. This person wanted to be close to the pastor and his wife at that time, I could not tell her that it would not happen. I just listen to her. She wanted to get close to my pastors and for me to be under her while she was on their level. I did not say anything. My pastors respected her but at the end of the day, I was their assigned minister. She was extremely high-minded at that time.

Another incident occurred living with this beautiful one. While at the park a total stranger came up to me and began talking to me. I was reading a book and did not want to be disturbed. The Spirit made me put book down, I had to deny myself to be used. Well, my higher degree, high minded roommate at that time came over while I asked questions related to the belief system, she was about to become a part of that I knew the answers too. It was a way of getting the young mother of twins to think about the belief system she was getting involved in. Jeus Christ would ask people often questions, He already knew the answers to get them to think about their actions or lack of actions. My high-minded friend answers the questions, I asked the young lady before she could answer, thinking I did not know the answers. My high-minded roommate did not know I had done a deep study on false belief systems and different dominations of churches. The Holy Spirit used me to question her as Jesus would do even though he already knew the result. My high-minded roommate got very frustrated that the girl was still talking to me, I did not have a theological Doctor's Degree like she did. She walked away in disgust. I did not allow that to move me, I continued to do what God wanted me to do, plant a seed. The young lady was going to convert to Islam and was going to go to the temple. This was her husband's belief, and he was giving her time to make up her mind. He had not educated her at all about their systems. At the end I told the young lady to do her own research on this belief before she makes a discussion and to do research on anything in life before making life-changing decisions.

After some time living with this high-minded beautiful lady, I noticed I could not pray in her house. Not disrespecting her dwelling (in the Black culture, you do not pray in someone's house freely. They may think you are praying evil things against them, but to do it while laying down to yourself, silently going to the bathroom or cleaning) I could not pray laying down, going to the bathroom, taking a bath, while cleaning. Total block. I could not read my bible and get spiritual revelation either. I knew something was not right. My cousin that is younger than me, told me to do a study on snakes' sense God deal so heavy with me and enemies by using snakes. I thought that was crazy and not of God, so I did not. I prayed and prayed and said God that do not sound right. That sounds like witchcraft. I waited and stepped out on faith but prayed that Jesus's blood covered me or warned me. I finally studied snakes and their personalities. During the study, the spirit spoke to me and said the devil knows so much about the believers, but they know so little about him, why not have educated yourself in areas to be able to minister to others.

All my life and at the time of most experiences mentioned in this book, I feared the devil. My first experiences in a Holy Ghost church, seeing people get delivered from spirits and illnesses, scared the hell out of me. Then every now and then, you will have someone get up and want to be seen and they try to deliver someone from demons and the very next week, the pastor and elders' women in the church have to perform deliverance on the same person that tried to deliver someone else because they wanted status. I never forgot what the pastor uses to say, "stay your hips in your own lane, see what happens the spirit leaves the person that is getting delivered; they enter you with all your own spirits, your battling, you end up needing deliverance soon after, you tried to be seen." I promised myself and God that he did not have to worry about me doing that. I will stay my hips in this pew. I ain't never doing that! Lol! I was terrified of what I saw and did not want nothing to get in me like what I saw happening doing healing and deliverance.

After studying the characteristics of snakes, the Holy Spirit started showing me the different things I had encountered in my spiritual walk that I was not aware of, or I was in the mist of. I was shocked and understood something that had happened to me in my past even the more. There was a particular group of snakes that lived on lime deposits of a cave that I studied. The cave floor was covered with thousands of small snakes or more. You could not even see the caves floor for snakes. The Spirit associated the cave with the lime snakes to the place where I stayed with the pretty faced lady. This was why I could not pray at all: laying down, bathing, going to the bathroom, cleaning, not at all whiles in that dwelling. I could not focus on my bible study at all. I could not get revelation when I read my bible. I am not the one to say that this person was a witch, but I found out, out of this experience that that person's thought and deeds were impure toward me because of jealous and God knows what else. She had the crack heads in the neighborhood watching me and I did not know it until the morning God told me to get the boys and get ready to escape and do not come back. I got up, the spirit told me to lay back down because she was going to double back to the house for something and she did and that is when I saw shortly after she left that a person on crack was walking back and forth in front of her house. I had to wait another twenty minutes, then the spirit said get the rest of your items and the boys in the car quickly and leave and do not come back. I did just what God told me. We moved into a house I rented on the Westside of town across the street from the neighborhood witch I discovered a year later.

Wow! I was still scared of the devil when I moved there too. Strange things happened to me in this house too. God gave me revelations of how I allowed the enemy to multiply over the years, and this is why I keep getting attacked. At that point, there was a turning point, I got mad as hell with the devil and said enough is enough. I lost my fear of him but not my caution of dealing with his wickedness and being careful not to think more highly of myself than I ought. The Lord fights my battle, I am nothing without my divine creator: God, The Holy Spirit and Jesus Christ. No one can get to the father but through Jesus Christ.

After this, I came out of the Afro-American churches for at least two years. Me and my son attended a predominantly Caucasian large church, we somewhat blended into the sense no one cared about our spiritual growth. Quite a few of them were not believers, they were just church goers. My son said he liked the church because we were not there long. The church service was for an hour and then we were out. My son and I were used to longer church services. I needed time to heal and to hear the preacher minister the word. I attempted to go to their Sunday school. This church setting for smaller groups were same tactics as the Afro-American Church, you see a new face, you try to read the new face to see if they may object to certain things taught and the leader of bible school in their deep ignorance try to keep other newcomers from connecting with the one that they think would cause a problem. Not spirit led. I could not get my son to go to his own age group class, and I was so glad I did not because of what I experienced in that class. I had my poker face on not be read by anyone. The presenter talked about once saved always saved, quoted scriptures, and then jumped to scripture dealing with how beautiful Satan was and how he got kicked out of heaven. Wow? Really? The women did not go into detail about the conversion process, living a lifestyle that is Godly but instead talked about you can do anything and still be saved, that God will take one into heaven. I know we are all humans and are not perfect but come on! What about the scriptures that dealt with blaspheming the Holy Spirit (lying to the Holy Spirit, getting so angry with the Holy Spirit to sin), what about suicide? I found this presenter to be painting a pretty picture, a crowd pleaser. She kept saying you cannot do anything that God will not allow you into heaven. The lady kept looking my way and I showed no emotions as if you were not going to read my expressions.

There was another African Black Woman in class. She came over to me out of nowhere, apparently, she was visiting the class for the first time too and she had a chaperone in tow. The African women began to kiss me on both cheek and speaking something I could not understand. It was an uncomfortable event for me. My stomach churned from other women kissing me so lightly on my cheeks, but God let me know he allowed her to see who I was in Him. She recognized his spirit in me. The presenter was concerned about encounter, she did not like it and tried to figure out if I was going to be troubled. The chaperone was upset too and as soon as the African women stopped acknowledging me, she wristed her away from me. I blessed the Lord for that God encounter and prayed for that woman not to get caught up in this almost cult like control. I never went back to Sunday school in that ministry. My son and I continued to attend regular service. I had to educate my son where there were discrepancies in that presenter's teachings. I was so glad my son did not want to go to his age group Sunday school, God only knows what they were teaching in there. I am a worshipper, so I enjoyed the music they played. I was not getting a full spiritual experience. It was like getting meat without all the sides. When it was time to leave, after attending for two years, tithing, and giving offering, I left and went back into a predominantly Afro-American church. This ministry was interesting. A woman is only to be acknowledge as a missionary. How crazy is that? The New Testament KJV states: "There is neither Jew nor Greek, there is neither bond nor free, there is neither male nor female: for ye are all one is Christ Jesus." In other words, God is not prejudice. They sparingly called female pastors Sheppard instead of acknowledging them as Pastors. There is no true healing and deliverance ministry going on inside where the dominant male Pastor keeps a tight control on his leaders and members. Women are used to do charity things outside of church. Very seldom is a women allowed to minister. People are going through so much and need the wisdom of a women as well a man to make it these days. A woman is built to carry more physically and mentally, who else better to do healing and deliverance services if God has anointed that woman. Men can too but I have only seen a few men God has equipped in this area as heavy as women. I know it is more in small churches but why not the medium to big churches? The bigger church talks about revival, but do they want to lose control over their members, for them to be completely free in the Spirit? God knows.

When I came to this ministry, I had already met my husband and did not know it. When I felt compelled to join the ministry despite how they valued women's gifts, I had a revelation. I did not know a few men had had their eyes on me. When we were told to go to the room to get information about membership, a guy a did not even know came from the other side of them room by passing a few other people to hugged me and say we are sister and brother now, I could have hauled off and punched this man. How dare you approach me and put your arms around me not knowing who I was, what my background was. That is when I said, "here we go." I am not bothering nobody why these spirits bother me like this?" Then I went to question my walk, God is there any residue from my past is on me that I do not know anything about? God did not say anything. This was a test that I did not think I was going to past without physical hurting some man. This man basically tried to be in my view, but I ignored him. Later another man seeks me out. He tried to sit by me. I am tall and he was truly short; total turn off to me but no attitude if he does not try that "God told me you were my wife foolishness." I would have told him firmly; you are mistaken but I will pray for God to send your mate. Then another man. I got frustrated; God I did not come to church for this foolishness. When my husband came to church with me everyone noticed, even the one who had picked me up to get next too. I guess quite a few men was upset. What God has for you is for you.

At times, my husband could not attend church due to his work schedule. The man that approached me originally in the room to get membership information kept hope alive and ignored the wedding ring on my finger. One night my God sister and I went to an event at the church. We were seated by one Black women of African descent and her husband, this woman looked at me as if she could kill me. I would not have noticed if the Holy Spirit did not get my attention to see her reactions on her face. I was seated next to her husband. So, I made sure I was not touching her husband in any way. She was very ignorant, small-minded creature for her looks and gestures. While into the service, her husband bumped into the middle part of my hip. I thought nothing of it. Then it happened again, so a scooted over because I am a nicely shaped woman. Then it happened again, a scooted over again, then he bumped my buttock. I was raging mad to the point I was going to ask him if there was a problem he had with his hand loud enough for people to hear. My God sister in Christ wonder why I was that up on her. She gave me a look like what are you doing, get off me. I gave her another look of anger. She then said "are you ok? And I said no. I got to the point where I made up in my mind if this man touches me one more time, I was going to knock his lights out in the Church house. At some point we were standing up and this fool did it again. Before I could react to my intentions, an elder that I respected from the ministry looked in my direction for some reason. He was not looking at me, he just looked in my direction. I did not hit the man or call him out for his acts. That was the second time God used that elder to keep me from punching a man's lights out.

Missed Friendships

I HAD OPPORTUNITIES to be great friends to women married to pastor but had to end it before it had a chance to developed into great friendships because her husband pastor made a pass at me. The co-pastor wife's husband and head pastor of their church held my hand for an extended period for no reason other than to get my attentions. I ended up snatching my hands away and looked at him as if you got the wrong one. I will not be your side piece or anything else. I distanced myself as soon as I became aware of the man's intentions. I would pray to God to keep the Pasters wives comforted and strong in God because I was not the first or the last women that these men would try to use. A man is not going to allow a strong relationship to develop with another woman he wanted and could not have. Any man does not want his woman to be close to anyone but himself anyway. The only relationship that I have witnessed in my life was my grandmother and my Godmother's close friendship. My grandmother loved my grandfather so much that she put up with his infidelity, his drunkenness and staying out. My grandfather desired my Godmother, and my Godmother would not give him the time of day, so he starts picking her children when he sees them out on the town.

My Godmother came to my grandmother with her pistol one time and told my grandmother that my grandfather had harassed her eldest daughter at the bar, and she came to put a hole in him. My grandmother peacefully said to her, he was just mad because you want to allow him to have his way with you. My Godmother never told my grandmother about the advances my grandfather made toward her, and she had never told her good friend because she did not want to hurt her. This was the only relationship that I know of lasted the test of time and as one can see who wants a relationship like that. It is awful for women not to be able to connect with someone to share things other than marriage issues with other women. Women in this area often feel alone and that no one else understands and know what they must contend with. This is the enemy game to keep women separated. Can you imagine how powerful a group of three cords is? Women's can be to the destructions of the kingdom of darkness. In my opinion and the type of women I have been around; many women do not trust each other. They have a challenging time communicating with one another, working together.

Witchcraft & High mindedness

I HAVE EXPERIENCED Witchcraft in the pews. Do not be so quick to think a person is taken in by the spirit of Christ when they are swaying and looking like they are drunk, especially if it is a woman. Women that have husbands working in the ministry are so jealous in their hearts and will practice controls spiritually in the pews, aka witchcraft. This had happened to me within the last four years when my husband was not able to attend church with me one morning. I was completely shocked. Here I am a seasoned warrior, loving person and watchful, was almost overcame by a woman spiritually in the pews. She never touched me, and she was not too close to me. After experiencing this I was mad. I was not the woman this woman's husband was eyeballing; it was my beloved cousin he was looking at and tried to be attentive too. But at the same time, it only reminded me not to think more highly of myself than I ought to. In other words, do not think that you are too strong not to be overcome by the devices of evil. It humbled me that the Trinity: God the Father, Son & Holy Spirit is my creator, and I am to stay dependent on him and not my own wit or strength.

I knew a stronger, older woman that someone close to her planted something in her purse. God allow me to see what this woman was going through alone. She had found two brown pennies glued together with strands of her hair between the pennies. I saw that she was having usual mental problems and that there was something else going on that God did not show me. While my older lady acquaintance was going through the above mentioned; God tested me, by sending a witch for me to minister too from time to time. The witch loved being around me. She was getting healed just by being in my presence for short periods of time. She practices WICCA. God led me to Baptist bookstore downtown Jacksonville to pick up a book the explained what WICCA was. I knew it was not of God, but I needed to know what I was dealing with. Anyway, I could only talk to her short periods of time while praying deeply to be covered by Jesus Christ's blood. The older lady friend, who had the glued tight pennies with hair in between them, asked me to ask this lady that practice Wicca, what the item she found in the bottom of her purse meant? My neighbor asked me if it was me that this happened too, and I told her no. She told me that the person was trying to drive my older lady friend crazy, this why her strands of hair was glued tight between the two pennies. She also mentioned that it also meant that no matter how much money came to her, she could not keep money.

The other detail that I could not see was the person was making her lose money and not keep money. My older, seasoned, well equipped friend stated that her mind was drifting at times. She felt like she was walking in a cloud. She went on to say that she could not keep any money, she was losing money either, forgetting where she hid it. She was having to pay for all kinds of unexpected charges such as usual charges on her phone bill. The Wicca lady went on to share with me that people can use fingernails to do things to you. She said when she goes to one of her close relative's houses, she makes sure she does not leave hair or nail clippings nowhere around that relative because she knew this woman did not care for her, she only tolerated her. Wow, do this ever sound familiar to my own current situation as I write this now. Praise God from whom all blessings flow. Getting back on point, when Wicca lady time was up, God let me know to put distance between us. While there is blood still running warm in your veins, you have a choice to turn from wicked ways and choose God and live on eternally in Heaven.

I saved an event for last. Over the years I was called cold from time to time. Family members & a previous relationship said that I did not have compassion at times. I did & I do. I do not condone or overlook irrational behavior. We all make mistakes. I do not understand how people at times sugar coat things others have done repeatedly. It is a waste of time. I am blunt at times and that can be taken as being cold-hearted. Adults must take responsibility for our actions. I lead in with this description of part of my personality to explain this part of my personality may be linked to my relationship with my mother. I loved my mother. We started out as being like sisters, but I knew she was my mother.

My mother never showed me any type of affection because she was raped by my father which was much older than she is. She was dating him in her 12 years of high school. I do not know if she was dating him out of result of combination of him being attractive and or him being aggressive. My father was an extremely dangerous man in those days, and he got what he wanted when he wanted it. My mother and I did not have a conversation about their relationship in-depth. It was too painful for her. I did not find out that I was a date rape baby until I was in my late thirties. I asked my mother over the years, as any normal child would, why she did not stay with my father? Finally, in my late thirties, she said, "He did something I did not like, and I did not like him anymore." She went on to say, "He forced himself on me and I begged him to stop and to take me home." I never figured it out over the years, and I know God did not want me to know until I was able to handle such knowledge. My mother was very hurt, for after all this was not the first time a man forced himself on her. She was raped by her brother in the sugar cane field when she was a young lady. There were other incidents that my mother never told me about, so she was incredibly careful when dealing with men.

When my mother spoke to me it was with a different tone than all my other siblings. I noticed this when I was a pre-teen. When she called them, it was with a loving tone and endearing tone. When she called me. It was with a matter-of-fact tone. I noticed it but it did not faze me. I know this was God who did not allow this to dig deeper to find out why. I did not care because I did not need all the attention my siblings needed, not even when I was a little girl, when my grandmother passed. I was very independent and loved to be alone to entertain myself. My mindset of when my mother told me I was a product of rape was so loving towards her. I could not imagine her, in her senior year of high school, being pregnant with me and she should be enjoying her last year of school. I could not imagine her having a baby out of violence, fear and then having to have me. My grandfather knew what happened and was truly angry about it and refused to allow my biological father to see me. He wanted to kill him for what he did to his daughter. I believe my grandfather had so much love and compassion for my mother that he had made up in his mind that he would raise me with the help of my grandmother.

My poor, beautiful mother. I imagine that my grandmother made my mother have me when she did not want too. My mother having to look at me and being a constant reminder of this man. My features were of this man. My skin tone is of this man. I should have been aborted but God! I am here today because of God's Will. God has used me to bring healing and deliverance to quite a few individuals. He has used my life to impact people. I am humble and have always been humble. When I talk to myself in the prior sentence, I repeat what others have said to me. A person once told me that when anyone come into my presence and be around me for a while, I evoke them to change, to become a better form of themselves. I did not understand why this person told me this. She explained that the anointing I carry, the way I encourage and carry myself motivates people to change and to go for their dreams. I am not supposed to be here! But God! I am glad to be here too. Thank you, God, for keeping here. I was to be aborted.

I Know I have been changed:

- I fell in love with myself when I turned forty. My motto for years after that was: "I love me some me." It is amazing that people say I love Jesus but do not love themselves. How can you love Jesus and do not love yourself?
- I had given so much to others and had not given anything to myself. I did not know what hobbies I liked at 40 years old. I always worked, never traveled. Still waiting on the trip. I started focusing on me and how to love me without sacrificing a substantial amount of my time and energy for others.
- I discovered making others happy and comfortable is not the same as making myself happy.
- I enjoy the simple quite time I can get every now and then. Love spending time being quiet and listening just in case God speaks to me.
- I can make a meal out of anything. When I was younger, I used to get nervous when I did not have the components of at least a three-course meal or what my ideal of a standard meal is. I would worry myself down until payday. Being hungry and homeless a couple of times in life teaches one that there is something in your dwelling that you can eat and be full of a glass of water. Sometimes, you just need to check your fridge or freezer and make a meal with what is available.
- I do not allow anyone to oblige me if I do not want to do something.
- I have no problem with telling people no and not explaining.
- I do not entertain unnecessary foolishness other people allow in their lives; do not waste my time listening to

them complain and they do not do anything about it. Time is precious and it do not make sense to waste it on drama that do not profit you or the kingdom of God. If I must accompany someone out of obligation and drama is going on, I tune everything out going on and do not get involved, waste of energy. I love people as God does but I do not part take in foolishness.

- I can see why God do not deliver people out of certain things because of the unnecessary drama they allow in their lives. I am a living witness myself of the poor choices I made in life. I have a great understanding & respect to why God did not deliver me.
- When I face a life's crisis: homelessness, hunger, prolonged usually physical illness, great losses in finance, Black magic, Witchcraft, voodoo, materialistic items or a beloved one, I turn deeply into Jesus Christ's bosom and stay there until I see the breaking of light. I meditate on Jesus Christ love for me. That is all I think until the yoke is broken, the test has passed, I can feel or see a rebound from my poor choices in relationships, financial and or business moves.
- Witchcraft, Black magic, Wicca, Voodoo or whatever you called evil if you are in the right standing with God, it will not prosper. The weapon can be formed and can try to destroy you, but you cannot allow it to intimidate you, make you sad "why God, why would someone want to do me like this, I don't bother no one." The situations may make you angry to fight fire with fire. Leave it in God's hands and rest. Soon you will be shown how God dealt with that person.
- When you shake hands with the devil, it will always cost you more than you think. He does not play fair at

all. God allows something to happened to break you, teach you something, get you out of that negative, destructive mindset. Also, of thinking more highly of yourself than you ought. Nothing can touch me. I am stronger than ever. Watch out! God will allow certain thing to show you who He is.

- I have been equipped to endure certain sufferings that occur in life from time to time without deep heaviness.
- I have more patient now than years ago in waiting on God to direct my path.
- At times, I have just enough patient like Moses had to have at, at the Red Sea when everyone turns against him and while on the journey, the people kept turning on him even though they knew in their heart, this was a pure upright man before God. He had a heart and well made-up mind to serve God. I have had quite a few circumstances that came against that I can relate to Moses, of how people know your heart but turn on you for no relevant reason.

www.ingramcontent.com/pod-product-compliance
Lightning Source LLC
Chambersburg PA
CBHW071858070526
44583CB00016B/1743